Fred

The Biography and Writings
of Fred Marks,
Baba's 'Grand Old Man' of England

COMPILED AND ANNOTATED

by

SUE CHAPMAN

2024 COMPANION BOOKS

I am that Ancient One whose past is worshipped and remembered, whose present is ignored and whose future Advent is anticipated with great fervour and longing.

♡

Introduction

I met Fred Marks once, at his home in Putney, West London, in 1984. It was an intimate gathering. I had come to Meher Baba the previous year and knew few Baba people in the UK. As I stepped into Fred's flat, away from the noise and bustle of the London streets, I had the impression of entering a still-point in the universe. Fred was seated on a simple, upright, 1930s dining chair. It was set against a wall, and it seemed as if he was trying to 'retreat' into the wall itself. His arms were draped across his lap and his head was bowed. As he gazed up at me from under his bushy eyebrows, I sensed a loving sweetness and deep humility emanating from his eyes. His seated posture belied his standing height of well over six feet, so my initial impression was of a small, slight man. Whilst we only exchanged a few private words, something of his presence was nonetheless luminous, and that profound impression remained with me thereafter. Now, nearly 40 years later, I am curious to find myself writing his biography.

On one of my rare visits to the London Meher Baba Centre in the '80s, I was told that Baba's chappals, on display in the Meeting Room, had been Fred's; given to him by Baba's sister, Mani and brought to the Centre after his death in March 1985. Naturally I was curious to know more about that; when and where, and why would this simple Englishman have been so blessed as to be gifted shoes that God Himself had worn? It seemed incredible to me, yet no one seemed able to tell me more. They were certainly the most significant Baba treasure visible in the Centre at that time, and the touchstone for all Baba's lovers passing through. Over the years, hundreds must have bowed down to them in the Basement Flat at 228 Hammersmith Grove in London. I didn't know then how much those chappals, and Fred's life, were to become a part of my own.

Don E. Stevens also plays a significant part in this story. With Murshida Ivy O. Duce, Don was responsible for publishing *God Speaks* and many other Baba books. He was one of Meher Baba's early Western disciples and was granted regular access to Baba during the fifties and sixties. Though working largely in the US, Don maintained a flat in London above the Baba Centre at 228 Hammersmith Grove, and he held regular Baba meetings there. When he passed, (26 April 2011), his ground floor flat was gifted to the Association. A decision was taken by the Board to refurbish both properties, and create an integrated, dual-level Centre that, in addition to the Basement Meeting Room, would afford a space for quietude, the display of Baba artefacts, and also provide room for archival work and storage.

Through volunteering in the MEM Archives at Meherabad over some years, I had learnt a little about conservation work from the experienced team there, so considerations about the care of MBA's Baba treasures suddenly and unexpectedly fell to me. For Baba's most precious chappals, we commissioned a display case that would offer good protection over the long term, whilst allowing full visibility. The chappals were thus rehoused when the Centre reopened in 2016.

It was only very recently while researching Fred's life, I learnt that the chappals had originally been given by Baba to Will Backett. Will and his wife Mary met Baba in Coombe Martin, Devon during Baba's first visit to England in 1931 and later spent time in Nasik, India with Baba during 1937. The chappals are similar in style to those Baba wore in India at that time. Finally, I was beginning to find the missing pieces of a Divine jigsaw puzzle.

Martin Cook sourced the photograph of Baba wearing this style of chappal. The Archive team in India told me that Baba

had a few similar pairs made over several years, so we cannot date them exactly. Suffice to say undoubtedly it was my curiosity about Baba's chappals that became the 'footsteps' on my journey to learning about Fred.

Baba called Will and Mary Backett *Wilmar,* and also described them as His Archangels. We must assume that the chappals came to Fred after Will died, as the two men had been the closest, brotherly companions in Baba. Fred kept them in a box at his home, keeping Baba informed of the storage conditions. He showed them to his many visitors, and for the rest of his life he also carried them to Baba meetings.

Whenever I handled Baba's chappals during the restoration project, I thought of Fred and found I was intrigued to know more about his life. In late 2021, we transferred the chappals from the Basement to the Ground Floor Flat, and once again my curiosity about Fred was piqued. It felt as if Baba was continually nudging me to learn more. I approached Lol Benbow, who was close to Fred, to see if he recalled seeing any notebooks at Fred's, and if so, what had happened to them after he passed? Amazingly, he remembered a lady called Victoria coming on one occasion and Fred giving her a stack of papers to take away. Lol said she was en route to California. Finally, I had the germ of a search.

I contacted Alan Talbot, a long-time Baba lover living there, asking if he knew a lady called 'Victoria' who travelled to London in the '70s or early '80s. It was a crazy long shot, but almost immediately he replied citing two possible people and suggesting I contact Ursula Reinhardt for clarification.

Ursula met Baba on her travels in India in the sixties and knew all the early Baba lovers and thus the possible courier.

I was very excited and wasted no time. Again, an instant response came. Ursula knew the person, and that Fred's writings were carried on behalf of Filis Frederick, the founder and editor of the *Awakener* magazine. Filis published articles about Meher Baba between 1953 and 1986, and as I later discovered, had requested some 'stories' from Fred. Ursula told me that Filis' archives were now in the care of Chris and Christi Pearson, and she suggested I contact them for further help.

Knowing Christi from visits to India and swept up in a field of energy so characteristic of 'Baba at play', I contacted her immediately. In His perfect orchestration, at the very moment my email landed, Christi was actively engaged scanning Fred's documents – incredible! In the space of a day, Fred's personal archives had been located for me by these helpful friends. This seemed to me perfect affirmation that Baba wanted Fred's memories, 'hidden in plain sight' since 1979, made visible. What a difference a day makes.

Now, with the possibility of repatriating Fred's writings, we might finally learn more about the person Baba's sister Mani called 'the Grand Old Man of England'. Once the scanning work was complete, Christi kindly couriered Fred's documents to Myrtle Beach and I was able to collect them there. The Meher Baba Association, (Friends of Meher Baba, UK) is hugely indebted to Christi for the time she spent scanning Fred's collection and for her willingness to release them. And that's how it was that Baba's chappals became the 'footsteps' to unveiling Fred's life.

Fred is compiled in Three Parts. Part One is Fred's biography, drawn from handwritten notes, transcripts from film footage and recorded talks, correspondence, and personal anecdotes. Fred's records were mostly undated, and in his recollections he jumps back and forth in time. For the ease of the reader, I have edited them chronologically as far as possible. Fred's narrative is found indented within the broad text. He was a 'turn of the twentieth century' man, with a somewhat Victorian manner of expression. Consequently, his language is more formal in construction than is now used. At the same time we should also be aware that Fred's formal education ended at age 16. Some minor editing of syntax has therefore been necessary, but to allow his authentic voice to speak in its own time, wherever possible, I have left his narrative untouched.

Part Two comprises extracts from the manuscript that was sent to Filis for publication. Fred titled it *Experiences* and it is presented in his distinctive hand. Some brief passages appeared in 'The Awakener', Vol 2 No.4. True to its title, it reveals Fred's *Experiences* gleaned from Discourses heard directly from Baba, and his thoughts intimated from living as His disciple. It is expressed uniquely from his soul self, much as a prayer of fervent love for his Beloved Baba. It has a timeless simplicity.

Wherever I was unable to attribute text and to avoid misquoting Meher Baba's words, some pages have been edited. A reader wishing to view the original in its entirety may do so by request to Friends of Meher Baba, UK.*1

Part Three comprises Appendices:

Appendix 1 - Keith Miles, a British Baba lover and collector of Baba books and memorabilia, learned I was working on *Fred,* and kindly shared a package of letters that had been passed to him for safekeeping after Fred died. They begin with Fred's earliest communication with Baba in 1946 and make a wonderful and significant addition to this biography, revealing Fred's sustained and loving contact with Baba's family and close Mandali throughout his life.

Appendix 2 - Fred liked to write poetry or prose and loved music. The English Arti, that the Mandali had asked him to compose, is reproduced along with selected poems. For brevity I have not reproduced them all, but as with *Experiences* they can be read on request. The couplets that appear throughout the book as Chapter headings were extracted from an extended piece of prose found unattributed within Fred's writings. We can only be certain that they were couplets that had meaning to Fred, whether from other sources or his own words. I have also included a brief play of Fred's that was brought to my attention by Scott Makeig who directed a production of it at UC Berkeley in 1972.

Appendices 3 & 4 are, respectively, Fred's Obituary and an Epilogue.

Baba lovers from the UK and US provided personal recollections of Fred and I have included these as Chapter endings throughout the book. They reflect most beautifully the impact Fred had upon each of their lives and thus reveal much about Fred's nature. I am grateful for their contributions.

Fred passed away on March 2nd, 1985, in the early morning, at the Royal London Homeopathic Hospital, Great Ormond Street, London, so this publication is long overdue but also exactly according to Baba's time. If any surviving relatives of Fred's siblings find this modest biography, I trust they will forgive any errors. Friends of Meher Baba UK would certainly welcome their contact.

Acknowledgements

First, my heartfelt thanks to Chris and Christi Pearson, without their work and generosity there would be no publication on Fred's life. I most deeply appreciate the tireless help and encouragement Richard Cork has provided as Editor. He steadfastly worked through the many stages required to bring *Fred* to completion, including undertaking the text layout, and his diligent help has been invaluable.

My sincere thanks to Christine and Martin Cook for their generous help with both original and reproduced photographic images. Sheila Krynski provided inspiration and much helpful advice at the outset. It was a joy to receive constructive input and encouragement from Heather Nadel who read the first draft of *Fred* and subsequently directed me to Sevn McCauley and Companion Books who kindly agreed to publish this edition. As Don E Stevens founded Companion Books, and my journey with *Fred* began in Don's flat, this outcome is particularly sweet. Thank you all.

My appreciation to Jesse Mednick and Meredith Klein at the MEM Archives in India for their historic guidance in archival work, and for researching and sharing document scans. My thanks to Naosherwan Anzar, David Fenster, Irwin Luck, Tony Zois, Philip Creager and Keith Miles, who all kindly offered, with permissions, publications or materials held in their personal collections. Their combined contributions form a significant part of this edition.

I am grateful to Rosie Jackson for editorial help on the Introduction and Fred's poetry, and to Celia Freije and Tony Howell for constructive feedback as readers. Diane Snow found the image of Fred at the American Sahavas and arranged permissions for use from Sufism Reoriented. Shelagh Rowling sourced Fred's family and war records. My thanks to Darren Turner for designing the book jacket.

Finally, may I especially acknowledge all the 'memory bearers' who willingly shared their experience of Fred, and by so doing, enable us all to have a deeper sense of him. Their stories appear at Chapter endings across the text. I hope together we have captured Fred and succeeded in revealing a measure of the significance and spiritual essence of a life lived entirely in service and surrender to Beloved Avatar Meher Baba.

Fred's life spanned two World Wars and much of the twentieth century. As an early disciple, Meher Baba called Fred to be one of His 'Fishers of Men' in the West. He faithfully fulfilled that mission, bringing Meher Baba's name to countless souls he met on his journeys around the streets of London, and in meetings he held over decades. How blessed we were to have had him in our midst, and to discover this legacy of his life immersed in Baba, a legacy that we hope will continue to inspire and endure for lifetimes to come.

Sue Chapman

Craster, Northumberland, UK

November 2023

Images

Photographs

All photographs kindly prepared for publication by Martin and Christine Cook.

Cover photo, and on pp.229, 'Three Incredible Weeks', 1954, courtesy Meher Nazar Publications, permissions this publication only.

Back cover courtesy of Martin Cook.

Preface, Meher Baba, 1954, photographer unknown, 'Oceanic collection of prints, Friends of Meher Baba, UK.

Meher Baba on Champa, c.1936, pp.4, courtesy of MSI Collection.

Meher Baba with Will and Mary Backett in India, 1937, pp.47 and 48, courtesy ECPPA collection.

Meher Baba and Mary Backett, Sevenoaks, England, 1933 or 1934, pp.50, Friends of MBA, UK.

Meher Baba at Wadia Park, 1954, pp.82, photographer B.Panday, courtesy MSI Collection.

Meher Baba on Seclusion Hill, 1947, pp.90, courtesy MSI Collection.

Baba with the Western Men, 1954, pp.100, courtesy MSI collection.

Baba leaving London 1956, pp128, courtesy Meher Nazar Publications.

Camera stills from East West Gathering pps.187,195,198 from Mani Irani's family films, courtesy Sheriar Foundation Inc.

Mehera, Meherazad, c,1970, pp.319, photographer unknown, 'Oceanic' collection of prints, MBA.

All photographs of Fred in London, and Mary Parry, Adi Sheriar Junior and the Great Darshan group kindly shared by Martin Cook from his private collection:

Pps. 2, 16, 73, 106, 137, 168, 173, 194, 216, 224, 230, 237, 248, 273, 350.

Photograph of Fred in Myrtle Beach, 1958, pp.140 shared by kind permission of Sufism Reoriented for this publication only.

Photograph of the Memorial Tower, Meherabad, pp.43, courtesy of Johann Noble.

Photograph from the 1958 Guest Book Register, Baba's House, Meher Spiritual Center, pp 136, courtesy of the Board of Directors.

Scanned documents

Fred Marks archive, Friends of Meher Baba, UK:

pps. 32, 36, 39, 41, 61, 70, 87, 108, 110, 111, 114, 123, 138, 139, 154, 181, 191, 192, 203, 253, 256, 257, 262, 267, 270, 271, 276, 278, 282, 284, 285, 288, 294, 296, 298, 300, 302, 305, 306, 307, 312, 313, 314, 344, 354, 355, 356, 357, 382.

MEM Archives, Meherabad, supplied by Jessie Claire Mednick for AMBPPCT: pps. 133, 215, 216, 217, 218, 219, 220.

Documents shared by Keith Miles:

pps. 19, 20, 54, 62, 64, 65, 157, 161, 177, 178, 179, 188, 231, 321, 333, 334.

Meher Baba - Lord of Mercy, courtesy of Philip Creager: pps. 164, 165, 166, 167.

Fred's war record sourced by Shelagh Rowling, pp 27.

Published by Companion Books

www.companionbooks.org

Table of Contents

Part One

Biography of Fred Marks
6th January 1900 – 2nd March 1985

It was favour from above made me ask my way of Thee,
and by eternal guidance I was led, Your face to see.

18

Chapter One - Early Years

If I cannot meet my loved one, I'm content to think of Him

Fred was born on 6th January 1900 in Basford, Nottingham, England. The Victorian era, which for decades had been characterised by glorious inventions, national and economic developments in many spheres, and a degree of world dominance, was gradually receding. Queen Victoria, once so revered, was at the very end of her more than sixty-year reign, forty years of which was shrouded by her widow's grief. The country was somewhat preoccupied with the Boer War in South Africa, and many were looking to the new century for transformation and the promise of a new era under a different monarch.

Nottingham had recently been granted city status, but that had done little to raise the levels of social deprivation that existed in many parts of this, then small, Midland's city. Whatever Fred's childhood experience, he sustained an affection for his hometown and revisited it with a younger Baba follower later in his life.

We know little about Fred's early childhood. The 1901 Census records Fred as the second born of his parents Louis and Alice, but in the 1911 Census another son aged 14 is recorded

XA 489827

194202

1 & 2 ELIZ. 2 CH. 20

CERTIFICATE OF BIRTH

Name and Surname *Fred Marks*

Sex *Boy*

Date of Birth *Sixth January 1900*

Place | Registration *Basford*
of | District
Birth | Sub-District *Carlton*

Certified to have been compiled from records in the custody of the Registrar General. Given at the General Register Office, Somerset House, London, under the Seal of the said Office, the 16th day of *July* 1954.

CAUTION:—*Any person who (1) falsifies any of the particulars on this certificate, or (2) uses a falsified certificate as true, knowing it to be false, is liable to prosecution.*

28/21/339

as the first born which makes Fred the middle child of a family of four boys – William, Albert, Fred, George, and one girl, Ethel the youngest. William was under two years of age at the time of the early census but appears to be in the care of another family member, possibly a grandparent, when the census was carried out. Louis' profession is recorded as French Polisher which would not have been sufficiently lucrative to support a family of seven, but it could certainly have had a bearing on Fred's later choice of profession in the antiques business since he would have acquired knowledge through his childhood.

20

The only family correspondence found in his papers was a telegram to Fred from Nottingham, dated 8 June 1970, from 'Bill' announcing 'Ethel's' death. Bill would have been his oldest brother recorded as William on the census. On the outside of the envelope, in Fred's hand, is written 'my sister'. Mary Parry, a fellow Baba lover of that time, writes in an undated letter to Fred that she will meet him at his sister's home in Nottingham, so that confirms Fred was in touch with Ethel long after he left home. Fred never married; we do not know if his siblings did. He may have had nephews or nieces, but none were mentioned.

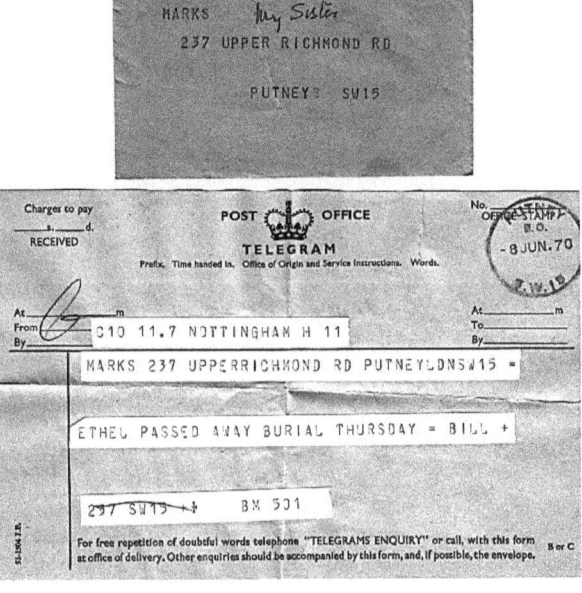

By the time those currently alive met Fred, he was so entirely absorbed in his life with Meher Baba that childhood recollections and talk of his family perhaps seemed irrelevant. Not one person approached could recall any family anecdotes. Therefore, my sources are taken from his early notes and comments drawn from his *Experiences* manuscript.

Describing his mother, Fred says:

> My mother was very poor but came from a prosperous Christian family.

Perhaps her family lost its fortunes, but regardless, she had married a man of limited means so life would not have been easy. Of his father Fred says:

> He was not religious, strict beyond the rule, and I with him was not a favourite. The hazards of experience when a boy taught me parental love and respect.

This somewhat understated, yet potent appraisal of Fred's father undoubtedly hints at some punitive handling, and an absence of affection between them. It certainly does not portray a model of family life that he might seek to emulate and, as his formative experience, it may well have contributed to his introspection and subsequent search for a deeper meaning in his own life.

Fred says he was raised 'in the Anglican tradition' which in the light of his previous statement, must have been a combination of his mother's influence and the schools he attended. We might assume Fred's childhood was navigated within a somewhat divided household where his mother and father held differing beliefs. His immersion in the Anglican faith is certainly reflected in the frequent biblical quotes and hymnal verses that pepper his writings. We learn that he was sent to a preparatory school at an 'early age'. Fred mentions that:

> Being of an impressionable nature, I often recalled to memory a large, framed text hung on the wall in the main hall of the preparatory school:

> Whatsoever things are true
> Whatsoever things are honest
> Whatsoever things are just
> Whatsoever things are pure
> Whatsoever things are lovely
> Whatsoever things are of good report
> If there be any virtue or any praise
> Think on these things.
> *(Saint Paul)*

> Those words remain somewhere in my memory over the years, but the deeply ingrained tracks of life's habits are not easily surmounted. The constant wheel

that motivates our lives grinds away relentlessly as surely as one day ends and another begins.

These early Christian verses may have heralded Fred's early spiritual awakening. He summarises the closing of his childhood as follows:

> There were no selfish interests by either the parents, or their sons, to either one or the other. We were 'tossed out' of the nest in late youth and each went his own way.

This revealing statement suggests that Fred believed if a family member needed or wanted to remain with another, it was an act of selfishness. This view may have predicated his future solitary life, and so we might assume that from his early teens Fred considered himself pretty much alone in the world. In a later journal entry, Fred mentions seeking a house 'suitable to accommodate visits by his mother', so evidently, they remained in contact, and she may have outlived his father; but there is nothing to indicate whether those visits occurred, and no further reference to either parent appears in his diaries.

Fred recalls:

> From early youth onwards, I had a longing

somewhere deep down which was always hemmed in by a pent-up yearning to understand life. At the same time, deep attachments and worldly involvements began to attract me like a mirage attracts a parched traveller in the desert. I had neither urge nor inclination towards spiritual aspirations, and because of expediency of duty my enthusiasm ebbed for searching further ahead for the meaning of life.

As for all young men of the day, Fred had little choice about his personal future. The country was drawn into a war which was to engulf an entire generation. Fred recounts it thus:

In my seventeenth year the First World War was sweeping over Europe. During this time, I was called to London from my hometown in order to join the army and was posted to what then was considered to be the crack regiment of the world, the Guards. Once I was on parade and called out of the ranks to be the 'King's Messenger'.

During the 1914-18 war, a singular incident happened during my government post. I was 18 years of age at the time, but those years held out such a precarious future that I scarcely had the intrepidity to look further ahead. One day, I was in the refreshment room standing alone. A young man of pleasing countenance had ventured into the building, by-passed the sentries, and came to me holding a small booklet and said, "this is for you". I smiled at him and slipped it into my tunic pocket without reading it. He seemed to disappear as suddenly as he came. His appearance was angelic, and I believe there are angelic beings in incarnation. At that time, I was self-conscious and sensitive to the demands of the responsibility expected from me in my military service.

(The charger given to me has endeared me to horses to this day.) But that booklet! One day almost 20 years later by chance I happened to come by it again and recalled the incident. The title was on the cover and in these words: 'I Am Kept'. Never during those years did I give a thought to 'omens', good or bad, but on reflection it seemed it was an act of 'Providence'[*1] working through a human agency. The 'Keeping' described in the booklet is similarly expressed in the 91st Psalm of David:

He that dwelleth in the secret place of the Most High shall abide under the shadow of the Almighty. I will say of the Lord, He is my refuge and my fortress – my God - in Him will I trust......

Because he had set his love upon Me, therefore I will deliver him. I will set him on high because he hath known My Name. I will be with him in trouble; I will honour him; he shall call upon Me and I will answer him. With long life will I satisfy him and show him My Salvation.[*2]

It is worth noting that the role of a Guardsman is to serve and protect the King, so perhaps Fred was being prepared for his later service to 'The King of Kings'! The message embedded within the 91st Psalm quite evidently became the bedrock for the life that was to follow.

> 'He that dwelleth in the secret place of the Most High
> Shall abide under the shadow of the Almighty.
> I will say of the Lord, He is my refuge and my fortress, –
> My God – in Him will I trust . . . . .
> Because he hath set his love upon Me, therefore I will
> deliver him. I will set him on high because he hath
> known My Name. I will be with him in trouble;
> I will honour him, he shall call upon Me and I will
> answer him. With long life will I satisfy him, and
> show him My Salvation'

From searches in war records, we learn that Fred enlisted in the Guards on 29th January 1918 and served until 20th August 1919. (*Some of his service may have been in France or Belgium*). It was a grim time for all and would have been life-changing on very many levels. By the time Fred emerged from the Great War, twenty million had died, a further twenty million were wounded, and Fred himself was discharged with ill health just as the war ended. No doubt he would have witnessed all manner of suffering. For a young man, with so few positive experiences to draw upon, it must have seemed a very dark and sad time.

Army World War I Medal Rolls Index Cards, 1914-1920 for F

In *A Moveable Feast*, Ernest Hemingway recounts receiving a letter from Gertrude Stein saying:

All of you young people who served in the war, you are all a lost generation.[*3]

The phrase 'the lost generation' became the epithet of the age, characterised as it was by cynicism, disillusionment, and anger, an absence of faith in traditional values and an abiding sense of deep loss.

28

Fred says:

The First World War upheaval came to an end in 1918, but it was followed by a strange pathetic gaiety caught on by the masses of people. Among them, and especially the poor, there was an emotionally softened restraint not to air nor publicise grievances and suffering. The re-sounding echoes of war victory elated the national pride. It had also softened the natures and sensitivities of those who had come through it. At the same time however, it only served as a superficial veneer to hide hidden scars.

Economically the western part of the world was drifting towards another crisis. The years leading to, and the aftermath of, the First World War culminated in both victor and vanquished alike, each having to face similar difficulties. The upheaval had become universal and in some extraordinary way the greatest of all empires was slipping out of its harness, away from the reins that had controlled it. The world leaders were driven to expediency, by-passing and hardly questioning the spiritual side of man.

I was released from the army and sojourned to my hometown, took a course at the University and

School of Art, and returned to London. It was at that time I rented a shop and lived in North London.

Writing years later with the wisdom of hindsight Fred subsequently reflected:

The period just described very briefly, stands as a fading panorama of world events, now almost forgotten. Yet it helps to bring out the point, which is that the greatest and smallest significance of anything and everything happening on earth is only to be understood and explained in the light of those spiritual forces which benignly bestir, awaken, and guide humanity in its pure progression towards its final goal. The word 'pure' here, is to be understood in its spiritual purity and, in its potency, may be likened to the propelling force of love at every conceivable stage, from the lowest to the highest level.

And so, wherever humanity happens to be, the holy name of Meher Baba echoes on mountain and in valley from the lips of saints and ordinary men. It is universal and silent, yet imperceptibly by-passing the form. It is reviving the spirit of man to its original pristine glory. All life flows from One source beginning-less and endless, and every heart, directly or indirectly, beats to the cosmic universal rhythm which is sustained by the love divine which flows from God the Beloved in the divinity of Meher Baba. Through gradual stages some of us become aware that we are all re-acting and responding, though at first perhaps painfully during the metamorphosis, to the beginning of a joyous new rhythm of life to which Avatar Meher Baba has stated man is the rightful heir.

> From darkness, O Lord lead us into light,
> From mortality lead us to immortality
> *Upanishads*[*4]

If ever one were to doubt the transformational power of Divine Intervention, here we see how a man of receptivity and awareness can take the darkest events of his formative years, that might well have left him cynical and broken, and reframe them through the spiritual revelation of Meher Baba's Avatarhood.

But let us return to the time before Meher Baba was awakened within Fred, to learn how he 'found' Meher Baba.

Fred recounts:

> The early visits to England by Meher Baba from 1931 to 1935 were intentionally meant to be unknown

to the public. It is stated He was laying cables, inner means, or spiritual channels of communication. This might also imply some spiritual work unknown but to Himself.

Some of the English newspapers gave accounts of Meher Baba's visit to England in mid-September 1931. He arrived on the 'SS Rajputana'. Another passenger on the same boat was Mahatma Gandhi, who would attend the Indian Round Table Conference which was being held in London.

Great events were taking place in an effort to solve world problems, and these were the news headlines in the daily newspapers. True, they belong to the world of day-to-day happenings, and even though some major events became historic, as time recedes, even they gradually fade away from the memory of man.

In life's stress and turmoil man needs a greater sustaining power than himself to resolve his own life. The fact that Meher Baba was in England became known to the writer through the newspapers. To the millions of people who may have read about him, he may have appeared to be just an ordinary person. Meher Baba granted several newspaper editors at Fleet Steet interviews. The records of each have been preserved. The questions put to Him, as might have been expected, were intellectually based, and moreover, questions to the nature of which man himself had never been able to find satisfactory answers. Perhaps therefore innocently enough some of the questions were posed as a 'trap'.

Fred's first draft of his early life from notes for Experiences

It needed introspect to feel intuitively that which Meher Baba wished to convey in His answers. They were simple and one-pointed. His mission, as it has now become known in the hearts and minds of hundreds of thousands, indeed maybe millions of people over the globe, is such that its real worth could never be conveyed by publicity but caught on from heart to heart.

So here the reader finds these rather modest understatements – that Meher Baba's presence in the UK became 'known' to Fred through the newspapers, and he understood that to recognise Him as God required 'introspect and intuition'.

Fred reflects:

> Although my parents raised me in the Anglican Church, as a youth I was drawn to Theosophy, primarily to understand the theory of re-incarnation which was triggered by the spark of understanding and the intuition which comes about through Baba's grace. The process may take seconds, or it may take years. Baba's Grace is, I believe, imperceptible in its working. One suddenly becomes aware, or it may take time to come about, and Baba, like a mother, plays hide and seek with His children.

In another journal entry Fred again refers to having read about Baba in the newspapers, recorded thus:

> More than impressions from without, in the first instance when I read the newspaper interviews Meher Baba gave in London, especially to the Daily Express, I was both intuitively and deeply impressed from within –

indeed, convinced as to who Meher Baba was. I was impatient awaiting the following day's interview between Baba and the editor and the most learned professor who had been engaged to cross-question Him as to His status and mission to the West.

At that time, I was a very worldly young man. My highest aspirations and noblest traits of character were spent in the pursuit of an aimless worldly life. I was convinced that the only real help would be by Divine Intervention and that had always been at the back of my mind. Yet when I read of Meher Baba in the London Newspapers in 1932, I was both impressed and deeply convinced that He embodied all the hidden, superhuman qualities of life that the heart or soul of man could ever long for. Since then, this conviction has sustained me throughout my life.

Baba had already drawn many early disciples during his 1930s visits, but it was not yet Fred's time. We don't know how Fred worked inwardly with that recognition over the next few years, but he records in his journals the moment when he finally embraced Baba inwardly as his Master in 1935:

At the time of my 'Conversion', I was residing at a house which was situated two miles northwest of

Oxford Street. The initial consideration in keeping the house was that I should be able to provide suitable accommodation for a visit from my mother in London. For no particular reason, I had decided to have my divan on the ground floor in the front of the house. It had been a habit from my earliest recollection to recite the prayer of Christ at the moment of retiring. It was quite formal, and it was the only prayer I knew. At the head of the divan, hung on the wall, I had placed a text. The author unknown, is said to have been inspired by the biblical quotation:

> With Thee is the fountain of life
>
> God be in my head and in my understanding
>
> God be in my eyes and in my seeing
>
> God be in my mouth and in my speaking
>
> God be in my heart and in my thinking
>
> God be at my end and at my departing [5]

The text was more than a soothing balm to my conscience. It was the outward expression of an inward longing, which my life had precipitated, and which now had reached polarity. Yet at 9:00 o'clock on the morning of June 15th, 1935, the 'Call' came for me to leave all and follow the Master. It was not the voice of intuition; it was the voice of the Master. I submitted my will to the Divine Will and proceeded to dispose of all I formerly possessed. Life became new, and my enthusiasm was now to live for the Master and spread His message of love.

In a separate handwritten account of this experience Fred described it thus:

> Here I consciously abandoned myself and passed through calm passed helplessly while I became through the mercy of God a recipient to His bestowed Grace.
>
> The benighted and painful past was wiped out to be followed by the spiritually new life, something I had never received before. From my earliest days I had always admired the hymn, which contains this line 'Hath the marks to lead me to Him?' God came to my rescue with the saving Grace of Jesus Christ.
>
> He spoke these sublime words:
>
> "Sell what thou hast, and follow me and these gifts shall be added......"
>
> I replied "Thy will be done."

He awakened my heart, and it became aglow with His Divine Love and caused me to forget my own individual existence, and with it came a descending peace bringing sweetness and confidence into life. With this infusion of heart and mind, all cares for those near and dear to me disappeared. This spiritual consciousness of heart and mind was not complete; but the result of the 'Divine Operation' was permanent, as was revealed to me later through various aspects of self-knowledge.

This is written with such clarity and simplicity, and we know from subsequent accounts that for Fred there was no going back. From the year 1939 onwards to 1945, the Second World War was sweeping Europe. We know Fred was living in the Charing Cross area working in the antiques business. He describes the locality as follows:

The radiance and effulgence of Baba's Divinity at this time seemed to effuse and generate within the environs of the centre part of London in the vicinity of Charing Cross. At East Challacombe Baba had met those whose paths He had already crossed. That farmstead may have served a temporary need. It seemed at this time Baba had been crossing my path many times. I knew of Him, and He had given me something over those years which endeared me to Him for the remaining years ahead. Yet I felt precariously poised. I was at grips with my materialistic self and an uncertain spiritual destiny. The environs of central London encompass almost every aspect of England's past and present, and the pendulum today swings unsteadily into the future. Perhaps the poise is quickened, slowed, or steadily maintained by Baba who alone can arouse the aspirations of one and all, and bring about their fulfilment also. Who knows?

All who have hovered at the threshold of the spiritual path, perhaps in fear and uncertainty, will resonate strongly with the state of mind that Fred articulates so beautifully. But what comes next draws him further on:

> During this period there was an appeal for blood donations. I entered my name, and the appointment on a Sunday was kept. The donor was required to enter a small hall at the back of the Police Station a few yards along a continuation of Charing Cross Road. *(I had not forgotten this event but perhaps I doubted my experience of it.)* However, the transfusion was carried out by a nurse, and I began to feel I was being drained. I could scarcely raise my arm to receive a cup of tea from the nurse. In less than an instant I beheld the manifestation of St. Francis. As the nurse was handing me the cup of tea, at the same time the hand of Francis left the cup and the vision disappeared. He had appeared in the brown tunic with cord around his waist. It was years after this incident that I read Baba had stated St. Francis had not re-incarnated in the Avataric period. Baba stated Francis was the only God Realised Perfect Master in the West.
>
> So here again, Fred receives a benediction that surely must have surcharged his spiritual longing. It

cannot have been much later that Fred recalls:

> About this time, I rented a shop in a turning just
> off Oxford Street. I was always interested in antiques

and works of art. This shop and the nature of the business did occur to me years later to be a meeting place of many karmic links with persons whom I had to meet in this life span. An afterthought was that there may have been a settlement of many karmic issues, of dues and demands. At this particular time, Baba was scarcely known to me, or was He? I was imbued with a strange passion to share in the ups and downs of my fellow human beings. I carried a heavy karmic burden. *[This is such a powerful aside. Did this relate to Fred's WW1 experiences? Ed.]* An afterthought regarding my state of mind found expression in the quotation of a framed text which I had placed at the head of my bed in the house where I lived in North London. This inward longing, striving, and yearning throughout my daily life indeed became expressed in these words:

Breathe on me Breath of God
Fill me with life anew,
That I may love what Thou does love
And do what Thou wouldst do.

Breathe on me breath of God,
Until my heart is pure,
Until with Thee I with one will
To do and to endure.

Breathe on me Breath of God

Till I am wholly Thine

Until this earthly part of me

Glows with Thy Love divine.[*6]

> Breathe on me Breath of god
> Fill me with life anew,
> That I may love what Thou dost love
> and do what Thou wouldst do
>
> Breathe on me Breath of God
> until my heart is pure,
> Until with Thee I will one will
> To do and to endure.
>
> Breathe on me Breath of God
> Till I am wholly Thine
> Until this earthly part of me
> Glows with Thy Love divine.

On reading Fred's journals, one has a strong sense of some impending revelation that was to unfold. Fred continues his reflections:

> At that time, I was warden at a shelter and received some of the air-raid victims. Each received a cup of tea and a blanket. Northwards of this shelter, at Charing Cross, at a distance of a few hundred yards, I was on friendly terms with an elderly person who conducted an antique business. Her name was

Madame Polli. She was a widow and had been educated in a convent in Belgium, became a refugee, and came and settled in England. She was a quiet, unassuming person and sold bric-a-brac, but neither of us discussed philosophical subjects. I was thus surprised when she related to me the following incident.

At almost nine o'clock one morning while she was about to open the shop, she had a vision in the 'waking state'. Christ appeared and she said to herself, 'Why this is Christ, and He has tears in His eyes!' As she raised the palms of her hands to her face, the vision disappeared, but as she turned to look out towards the street through the shop window, on the far side of the pavement she noticed Meher Baba slowly walking in a Northerly direction with one of the Mandali on either side of Him.[*7]

We must assume from subsequent references that Fred and Madame Polli established regular contact thereafter though Fred only refers to her directly once again, to quote something she had said to him that remained in his memory:

When thou shalt stand with Him face to face,
Do not lift thy eyes,
For sight is vain in that holy place,
And the vision dies.

I have not been able to find a published source for this verse, maybe Madame Polli penned it herself. I wonder if those words were ringing in Fred's ears as we see him in the film 'Meher Baba's Call' approach Baba, head bowed, to receive His Darshan.

We cannot know the significance of Madame Polli's role in Baba's work during World War Two or thereafter, but Baba requested that her name be inscribed on the Memorial Tower at Lower Meherabad.[*8]

Photograph courtesy of Johann Noble, Meherabad

The link between herself and the Backetts was to have profound significance for Fred:

It was in her shop I first met Will and Mary Backett who were with Baba in Nasik in the Thirties. I distinctly remember Will saying to Mary, "Well here's Fred"! (*As if we had already met.*) From then onwards they invited me to their home at Halstead, Sevenoaks, in Kent and I became a regular visitor.

In *Lord Meher*, Bhau Kalchuri records that this meeting was in 1938.[*9]

Speaking of Mary, Fred says:

> The latter had previously said that Baba had given far more in the space of a few seconds than what she had gained in years of earnest seeking, for Baba can bestow Divine Love, whereas others can only talk about it.

Through Will and Mary, Fred was to meet Delia DeLeon, the founder of the English Baba group which was known then as the Meher Baba Spiritual League. Will oversaw the pan-European correspondence which at that time first arrived in England from Mani, Baba's sister and Secretary.

Finally, after many years of longing, Fred was drawn into the close circle of Baba's early Western Disciples, but it would still be many years before he would meet Him face to face.

***

Jan Coutu:

Fred was one of the first of Baba's western devotees that I met, I think in 1978. It was at the Baba Centre at Eccleston Square on my first visit there. Fred was very measured and thoughtful in the way that he expressed himself. He was a lovely, kind man and he carried himself with a certain dignity.

I also visited Fred at his home in Barnes, and my sister went to his weekly meetings. To me, Fred was like someone out of the Bible, devoted to His Master. He always had a quiet Presence about him, an aura of calm.

Chapter Two - Will and Mary Backett

The theme of my tongue for life's solace is His name,
The moments fly by, but I repeat the same.

Fred maintained close contact with Will and Mary Backett in the following years, and their importance cannot be overstated in their role fostering Fred's developing relationship with Baba and in introducing him to many of His lovers including Dr. W. Donkin, and Delia DeLeon. It seems important to include his notes about Will and Mary, their role in Baba's work, and his record of some of the ongoing activities occurring during the 1940s and 1950s in the UK.

In *Reminiscences* Fred records:

> Under Baba's supervision at Nasik, India, the Eastern and Western disciples mingled together in selfless service, thus brotherly and sisterly understanding became the sole media and bond of love in Baba's Universal service. Will Backett explained how, while in Nasik, he was overcome by the Indian heat, and so he retired from the work on hand, sat on the ground and supported his head in his hand. The devotees were preparing small bundles of cloth and food for distribution to the poor. Will however was anxious lest the work should be delayed.

At that moment, Baba happened to pass and touched him on the crown of the head with His forefinger. He immediately felt restored and recommenced the work which was finished on time.

Will and Mary, Nasik 1937 – Mary on far left, Will in solar topee.

When Will and Mary returned to England they lived at Old Oak Cottage, a well-constructed house, remotely situated in Kent, some thirty miles from London. Part of the road leading up to the house is narrow and strewn with boulders. Baba was on a visit to their house maybe in October 1933 or more likely June 1934, and as usual Baba was wearing sandals. He was accompanied by Will who commenced to remove some of the obstacles, however Baba immediately drew his attention and intimated that they should remain. Will attached some hidden meaning to the incident.

Baba with Mary, 1937.

A devotee who happened to be present at the house was a broadcasting musician. He was about to entertain Baba with piano music and commenced with the piece called *Oh Lord, what a Morning!*, but Baba switched him over to the tempo of the song called *John Brown's Body* [*1]

There was a steady flow of visitors to Old Oak Cottage. Amongst the regular weekly visitors of Baba devotees were Ann Powell, Madame Polli, the Kotwal family, living in Southampton, Homai Karkaria from Poona who was working in engineering in England, and Dr. C. D. Deshmukh of Nagpur, India.

Everyone, irrespective of status or importance, received the utmost considerate attention and service as though the person might have been Baba Himself. Visitors arrived from remote parts of England, Europe, USA, and India.

Will was responsible for keeping many European Baba devotees regularly informed of Baba news and messages, and because of the circumstances and nature of the work, sometimes urgent cables, instructions and messages arrived from India requiring in every instance minute attention to every detail for distribution over a wide area. For Baba's cause, he happened to be an adept without parallel for this work in England.

Baba asked if Mary and Will would like to move

nearer to London to live. She replied that the strain would be too much for Will. Ann Powell moved over

Baba with Mary at Old Oak Cottage, Sevenoaks.

the years between London and Wales. Madame Polli had airplane flights to Italy, and for Baba devotees and lovers in general it was a time of unsettlement in London. One Baba devotee, *[later established to be Fred though he eschewed writing in the first person. Ed.],* took a small bungalow near Canterbury, obtaining a job at St. Edmunds school as a teacher to the sons of clergy.

One day an order came via Will (*from Baba*) for devotees to go out and feed one poor person: the food, if possible, to be direct from the devotee's hand to the recipient's mouth. Here is a reference from 'a Baba lover's diary'. *[Again, this was Fred. Ed.]* On Sunday I peddled my bike for hours, going miles around in circles hardly meeting a single person. Then a woman appeared somewhere near Canterbury. I alighted the bike quickly and mentioning Baba's name asked her if she would like some food? She affirmed, and I put the food to her mouth, but was so anxious to carry out the order, that I realised afterwards I might have been more graceful.

This memory of Fred's reveals much about his determination to fulfil Baba's orders. In those days, in a rural location in England, this action would have been not only counter-cultural, but extremely awkward. For a bachelor, who struggled to even speak in the first person, to feed a woman, almost impossible! Yet he persisted.

Continuing in Fred's own words:

The Backets both visited a Prison but did not gain admittance, but it was followed up with a long correspondence to get Baba's books into the prison. Also, Will engaged an English national Sunday newspaper in a long, drawn-out correspondence pointing out the implications of the science of the age and the public's response was so great that the Editor committed to him the responsibility of taking over the correspondence. Thereby Baba's messages found an inlet into people's hearts and minds. These activities apart, both Will and Mary were pillars of strength to the group of 'Friends of Meher Baba in England' formed by Delia DeLeon at Baba's behest.

At a meeting of twenty-five invited women scientists, Will deftly pointed to a large chart from *God Speaks* by Baba and explained in the most erudite, yet simple terms the stupendous responsibility placed in the hands of the scientists and the rebounding effects on the subtle plane in the event of abuse. Will and Mary drew a gathering in the early 1940s of nearly 400 people to see a Baba film at Westminster House. They had all received a personal invitation.

Eventually orders came from Baba to His devotees, and amongst instructions to be carried out, property was involved. Old Oak Cottage was sold and after a weary round of searches, Will and Mary settled into a small bungalow in West Acton, London. Their work for Baba's cause increased and the postman who delivered the mail was given the name of 'God's Postman' by Baba Himself.

Sometimes special meetings would enable aspirants to come closer to Baba through being enabled to see photographic slides projected onto a screen showing Baba in seclusion, or bathing lepers, giving prasad or public darshan in India. Mary said, in effect, Baba's Manifestation to the world could not take place until His devotees had spread His Universal Message.

The following letter from Will Backett to Fred, dated 27/4/61, demonstrates their on-going work to purchase and distribute Baba's Universal Message. It details two differing quotes from printers and Will invites Fred's determination on the next print run of 1,000 copies.

When Baba's *Discourses* arrived, compiled in English by Dr. Deshmukh, some devotees were already aware of certain of Baba's gestures and His tendency to repeat actions, similarly where He wished to stress certain words. He would sometimes repeat them two or even three times in the *Discourses.* Mary copied the complete *Discourses* in her own handwriting as originally imparted by Baba to Dr. Deshmukh.

10 Westfields R⁰
N3.
27/4/61

Dear Ted,

I have just had a quotation of £5 for 1000 copies of the Universal Message in its original form as issued by Adi. This is from a local firm — Shakers quote £8·10 — for identical work. Do let me know if you wish to have them at the £5 quote. as soon as convenient.

Jai Baba

with love in Baba,

as ever

Will

acom
5434

Have you sent your paper?. Phyllis Frederick yet?

Now living nearer central London, Will and Mary were easy of access to meet the ever-streaming variety of work for Baba's cause. Visitors from Greenland, USA, Europe and many who heard of Baba for the first time came to visit them, besides visitors from distant parts of England. Baba photographs were on view and Mary would always listen to the guests with superhuman patience as she always felt visitors invariably wanted to unburden themselves of the pressures of life. Their home, Baba's home, had an atmosphere pure and serene, the surroundings simple and beautiful.

Sometimes Will would read a letter to regular visitors, and a letter from Mani which often contained some endearing message from Baba Himself to someone present, as though carried on a breeze to the recipient. Many went away refreshed and comforted with the words from Mary: "I am sure Baba will help you". They always disclaimed any credit saying, "it is not us; Baba does the real work."

Will was small in stature, Mary even more so. For years she occupied a cold damp room and almost suddenly became crippled with arthritis. It has been said of her that she was Madonna-like. Towards the closing years of her life, she resembled in appearance Baba's first Perfect Master and woman Saint of Poona, Babajan[*2], and ever exuded the excellencies of purity and childlike simplicity. Mary's birthday was the day and month of Baba's, February 25th. She passed over at the age of 86 years, in 1962 and was cremated. Will sojourned to live near Oxford until his passing later the same year. A remark made by Baba to His dear Will when he was at Meherabad on the Hill was, "Will, you are the machine of My heart."

It would be hard to imagine a greater tribute from the God-Man to one of His lovers.

***

Michael Lakey remembers Fred:

I met Fred at the old Eccleston Square centre in 1975, at an impromptu function being held there. He invited me to his, then privately rented, bedsit accommodation on the Upper Richmond Road near Putney, SW London. He always had Baba's sandals on the table with the sliding glass lid open and a plaster cast of Baba's hand on the wall behind his chair. I took the, now widely circulated, photo of Fred in a decidedly un-ironed shirt, sitting beneath it. I always left Fred's company feeling uplifted and any problem in my life that I had raised with

Fred seeming insignificant or put into proper perspective. 'It's all illusion you know', as he used to say.

After first meeting Fred we exchanged a few letters (lost now, sadly I think) when I was working at the Post Office, having moved to London after hearing of Baba through a library lecture by Mike Da Costa in Lancaster in late 1974. I wrote to Fred, mentioning that I was enjoying card games with some of the other staff. Fred replied, writing, 'Don't play cards with worldly people, Mike'. (Worldly people was a common phrase he used).

He revealed he was born in Nottingham and had worked as an art teacher, a dentist's assistant near Sloane Square, a King's Guard at the Palace and was in the antique business alongside Baba's brother Adi.

Fred was never married and when I asked him about past romantic relationships, his reply, which I recall well was, 'those whom I liked, they didn't like me; and those whom I didn't like, they liked me'.

Fred lived quite a solitary life but also received visitors from among the international as well as the English Baba community. He would also quite often venture out alone on public transport into central London, where he would inform people about Baba, sometimes using placards, leaflets, and posters. John Horder, the writer, first heard about Baba through

Fred in one of the Lyons Corner House tea rooms in central London.

Fred would even get himself on the radio via LBC's live phone-ins with Brian Hayes, to promote Baba in his own inimitable way. He went under the pseudonym of Charles but was eventually banned, or more accurately excluded, from getting through to the presenter on air. He also used to attend meetings at the Quaker Friends' House opposite Euston station, where he would tell the gathered assembly about Baba. Fred told me once that one of the group responded to his talk saying, 'The fool says....' to which Fred responded, 'the problem is, I'm not enough of a fool'.

Fred related that prior to hearing about Baba through Will and Mary Backett, he was on a desperate spiritual search based on a strong inner conviction that Christ had returned. He even mentioned going from place to place in London looking for the individual whom he could sense was Christ; such was the desperation of his search. Fred mentioned Will and Mary as being the perfect hosts and immaculate examples of Baba devotees in terms of kindliness and thoughtfulness.

He related that society could turn one into a kind of 'mast'[*3] and said that, once, he stood on a busy London street-corner giving money away to complete strangers, so disgusted was he with the world at that time.

Chapter Three - Meeting Meher Baba, London 1952

Our Friend is with us, wherefore then should we seek more than this?
The treasure of His converse is to our fond hearts sufficient bliss.

Fred continued for some years working in Canterbury, keeping contact with Will and Mary. Despite contacting the school where he was employed, they could find no record of him. He recalls:

> At this time, I was very restless spreading Baba's message. I hadn't met Him, but He wrote to Will Backett saying He knew of the work, and how I was working on behalf of His cause. I'm one of those whose nature feels Baba when far away from Him. The paradox is that He is always with us, I mean physically. For some reason some of us feel Him and we have more experiences either this way or the other. Having felt the love of Meher Baba I had one desire to spread His message, and since my background was in the Christian religion, I began to get an insight into the other five great religions of the world and discovered that the founder was the same again.

In *Experiences* Fred writes:

In Kent I continued contacting religious and prison centres. Sometimes I would display a scriptural message in the Main Street and encouragement often came, as little children would steady the arm of a parent as they would be passing hurriedly along. This in turn brought a deeper significance as the child would pause and read aloud the simple Divine invitation. Here I felt the Spiritual Presence.

Being a complete stranger to this city *[Canterbury. Ed.]* I prayed more intensely and deeply, feeling inadequate to cope with the apparent indifference, and I also frequently visited London at the weekend and broke the journey by calling on Will and Mary Backett, who always offered genuine hospitality. Will would also read to us some of the *Discourses* of Meher Baba, and I always came away uplifted and inspired.

On the point of leaving Canterbury, I again began to pray with more feeling. In due course a telegram came from Will to inform me that Jean Adriel had arrived in England from America and would be on her first visit to Canterbury. I had heard of Jean Adriel, whereupon at our first meeting she informed me that Meher Baba had told her to give me the book *God Calling*[*1], in which these words brought to me great comfort.

Fred quotes from the book:

"I always hear your cry, no sound escapes Me. Many, many in the world pray to Me, but oh! how few wait to hear Me speak to them, and yet to the soul, My speaking to it matters so much. My words are Life. Think thus, to hear Me speak is to find Life, and healing and strength. Trust Me in all things. Love showered on all brings truly a quick return. Just carry out My wishes and leave Me to carry out yours. Treat Me as Saviour and King, but also with the tender intimacy of the One Much Beloved. Keep to the rules I have laid down for you, persistently, perseveringly, lovingly, patiently, hopefully, and every mountain of difficulty shall be laid low, the rough places of poverty shall be made smooth, and all who know you shall know that I your Lord, am the Lord. Shower Love."

It is hard to imagine how significant and uplifting this message, sent directly by Beloved Baba to Fred, must have been. Fred continues:

Meher Baba issued an invitation to all His followers, disciples, devotees, and aspirants to write to Him direct. This invitation was issued through Will Backett, and I felt elated at this privilege. Shri Meher Baba has been in silence since 1928. The reply to my message was extremely brief and was dictated to one of His close disciples through the medium of His alphabet board. The words conveyed in it stirred me deeply, they were so charged that they reached beyond my expectations. The Master also stated He knew how I was working for His cause. I feel entirely dependent upon Him and know that I myself can do nothing.

Two early letters were found amongst Fred's archives, either of which may well be the response Fred was referring to. The first was sent by Adi K Irani on Sept 9th, 1946. It reads:

Dear Fred Marks,

Shri Meher Baba received your letter of 15th June. I regret the delay in sending you a reply. I was travelling all along with the Master in the Himalayas.

Any activity or devotional practice undertaken with the sole view of uplifting our fellow men spiritually, irrespective of self-importance or name, is permissible by the Master. For a specific method in the case of individuals, it is best revealed by the Master when interviewed. There is no knowing when He will visit the West. For the inflow of Baba's Love, one should resign completely all his actions in life to the firm conviction of doing everything for Him. As a child resigns to the treatment of its mother's love and care, the pupil resigns to the Master. Distance and lack of personal contact may not be necessary barriers to become the recipient of His Love.

With the Blessings of Baba ever on you,

Yours brotherly, Adi K. Irani

ADI K. IRANI .
Secretary
Meher Baba Publication Committee

King's Road
AHMEDNAGAR

Sept.9, 1946.

Dear Fred Marks,

Shri Meher Baba received your letter of
15th June. I regret the delay in sending you
a reply. I was travelling all along with the
Master in the Himalayas.

Any activity or devotional practice undertaken with the sole view of uplifting our fellow-
men spiritually, irrespective of self-improtance
or name, is permissible by the Master. For a
specific method in the case of individuals, it is
best revelaed by the Master when interviewed.
There is no knowing when he will visit the West.

For the inflow of Baba's Love, one should
resign completely all his actions in life to the
firm conviction of doing everything for him.
As a child resigns to the treatment of its mother's
love and care, the pupil resigns to the Master.
Distance and lack of personal contact may not be
necessary barriers to become the recipient of his
Love.

With the Blessings of Baba ever on you,

Yours brotherly,

ADI K. IRANI

The second message was an aerogramme addressed to Fred when Baba was sequestered at 'Kohinoor' in Hyderabad, and it is dated June 1st, 1951. Penned on Baba's behalf it reads:

Baba's Reply:

'Dearest and most loving Fred, your simple yet ardent letter deeply touched My heart. I know with what selfless love you have been, and are working for Me, and it is those rare ones such as you are who bring

Me so much happiness. My love to you and to all
those near and dear to you.

Baba.'

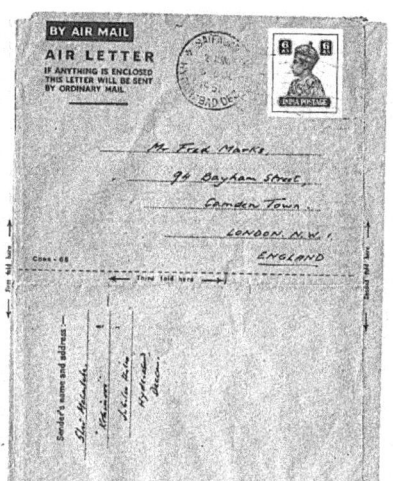

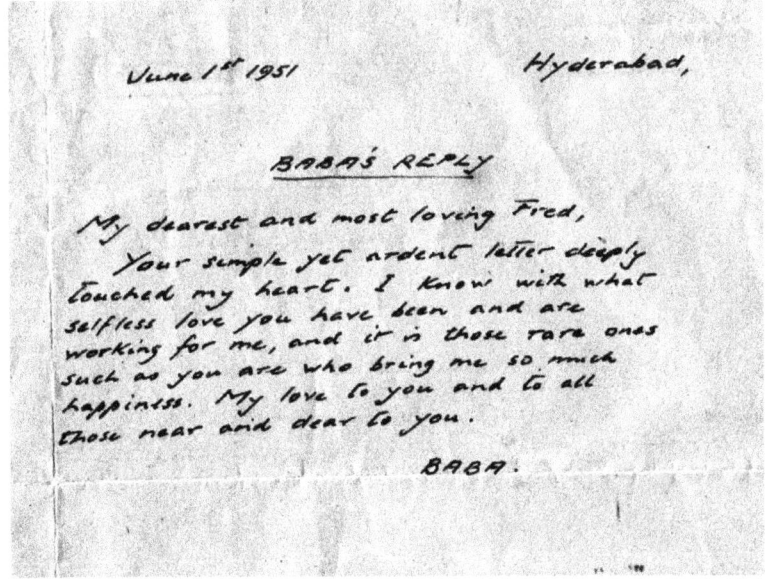

From 1960 onwards letters back and forth from Fred
to Adi and Jal became frequent, but these early ones, before

Fred had even met Baba, must have been so intensely precious and encouraging. Fred writes:

I recall a meeting which was extended to me by Will Backett at their cottage in Kent, at which Dr. William Donkin was among others present. This disciple has never left Baba and came with His permission to visit his invalid mother. At this meeting, among other things said, Dr. Donkin made a remark which to me was outstanding in my memory, when he referred to Meher Baba's relentless attitude to His close disciples in the carrying out of His orders and he said: "I believe His mercy is without depth."

Meher Baba sent word that He would visit London at the beginning of August 1952. This message was conveyed to his Western disciples and followers through Will. It never occurred to me with any certainty that I would be able to see the Master face to face.

"When man sees Me with his human sight it does not mean of necessity that his spiritual perception is greater. Contact with Me is not gained by the senses. Remember this to cheer My disciples who have never seen Me.*2

That Fred records this quote in his journal speaks to the humility that all who encountered him in later years experienced. He clearly took it to heart and in later years never made another feel that he thought himself more special or elevated for having met Meher Baba. On the contrary, many commented that he strove to meet them at their level and humbly offer what he could of his unique experiences. Fred writes:

> It is recorded that in India people flock to Baba in multitudes to be near to Him. The Divine purity of the Master affects and purifies all those who come to Him. Behold! The Eternal is in our midst, the priceless gift to mankind. The gauge and standard of which all humankind can be.

One cannot imagine Fred's feelings in anticipation of meeting Meher Baba after seventeen years of conviction and longing. Somewhat surprisingly, unless other accounts have been lost in time, he documents little of the worldly details of his meeting with Baba! No exact date, or time of day, just 1952! But much can be gleaned from other's accounts. When Baba and His party of men and women Mandali arrived from the US in 1952, all were still recovering from the automobile accident of 24th May in Prague, Oklahoma. One intention for their stay in London was for further rest and recuperation before continuing East, and for Beloved Baba to consult with an orthopaedic surgeon so that He might have His plaster cast removed. Baba and the women arrived from New York at the close of July, the men Mandali following on 1st August.

Despite His continuing pain, Baba had asked Will Backett to arrange a series of morning meetings at the Charing Cross Hotel so that He could meet new people. A programme of social activities had been suggested by Baba and arranged by Delia DeLeon, Will and others, especially for the women Mandali. Baba wanted to bring cheer and relaxation to them after what had been a very distressing time. Baba also participated in many of these events.

> 'Among those who met Baba for the first time were Tom and Dorothy Hopkinson, Douglas, Molly and Anne Eve, and Ken and Alice Lawton and their family.'[*3]

It is highly likely Fred's first meetings with Baba were between the 3rd and 5th August since Baba left for Zurich on the 6th. We know Fred met Baba in the Charing Cross Hotel then. He may also have met Him at the Rubens Hotel in advance, in the role of assistant to Will Backett, who was arranging the meetings. His brief account of these reads as follows:

Those who came for interviews were called singly, or in twos, from the large reception room up the wide stairway to the room occupied by the Master on the first floor. As I sat at Baba's feet, I was conscious of deep personal defects. I had anticipated something had to happen within me first if I was to receive more of His Grace. I have read all Divine things are received in silence. In His Presence the fool is speechless and the wise are silent.

During these two days, the disciples were frequently leaving the room, remaining just outside and then returning at short intervals. I heard the following year this was because the outpouring of Spiritual Light and Divine Love from the Master was over-powering. The vicinity was pervaded by an unutterable atmosphere of peacefulness. Aspirants, disciples, followers, and devotees were continually arriving, and some not scheduled turned up also from distant parts of the world.

The day following, I felt the need of INWARD help and was moved inwardly. Also, I remembered a gift which I had saved for the Master. Mrs Deakin prompted me to bring it along, whereupon I placed it just outside Baba's room and informed one of His disciples and again resumed my duties as doorman. Baba called me in to bring the gift to Him. Again, He pointed for me to sit down at His feet and taking my hand in His He looked extremely pleased. Baba's face beamed with laughter, and He said He was very happy. Baba said: "I am in Everything", and then added, "I will help you with My love".

The day following I felt the need of INWARD help and was moved inwardly, also I remembered a gift which I had saved for the master. Now I prompted me to bring it along whereupon I placed it just outside Baba's room, and informed one of his disciples and again resumed my duties as door-man.

Baba called me in to bring the gift to him. Again, he pointed for me to sit down, at his feet and taking my hand in his he looked extremely pleased.

Baba's face beamed with laughter and he said he was very happy.

Baba said

" I AM IN EVERYTHING "

and then added.-

" I will keep you with my love "

Fred Marks,

It is curious to me that I could only find three first person paragraphs about this long-awaited meeting with Beloved Baba. Even in Purdom's *The God Man* almost nothing is recorded of those brief days in London that were to be so life changing for many, but perhaps they have yet to come to light.

***

Keith Ashton, one time Chairman of MBA,UK and now residing in Cornwall, remembers Fred:

In the early 80's, seven of us would gather at Fred's tiny flat near Putney, London, for our regular weekly meetings, which were harmonious, friendly, and calm and always ended with the 'mandatory' cup of tea with cheese and salmon sandwiches. The theme was - 'Baba in daily life.'

I had several 'non-adventures' with Fred - here are three of them:

It happened that Fred and I decided to do a day trip to Brighton, which is a seaside town in the south of England. Fred was an expert in creating small bags of goodies and he prepared some for our journey: 2 bags, 1 for each of us, each containing 4 cheese and cucumber sandwiches, and an apple and banana - very English. When we arrived in Brighton, Fred wanted to have a clear view of the sea - the English Channel. In those days - early '80s - parking wasn't as 'severe' as it is nowadays, and we sat in the car eating the contents of our mini hampers, in silence mostly, simply staring at the sea - time stood still. After a while, and without ever leaving the car, Fred said — "Let's return to London" - and so we did, just like that.

I used to visit my sons monthly in Bournemouth, on the South coast. I would become very tired, due to stressful circumstances and the distance of the round trip, so on returning to London I would visit Fred for consolation. We would sit opposite each other across a table, and I would fall asleep for exactly 45 minutes - always 45. On waking, Fred would ask if I would like a sandwich and a cup of tea - my heart was so happy to hear those comforting words. He was truly a very kind and loving friend to me.

Another time, we were driving on Kensington High St near the centre of London - heavy rain was pouring down and the windscreen wipers were at double speed, when suddenly the engine cut out amongst very heavy traffic. Seemingly without thinking, Fred advised me not to try to restart the engine and we sat quietly whilst car horns were blaring. After the longest 60 seconds or so that I had ever experienced, he nodded. I turned the key and the engine started - such relief! Did Fred know something about carburettors?

When Fred met Baba at the Reubens hotel opposite Buckingham Palace, Baba said to him - "You know who I am". Baba also said that Fred was a "big man" and that "you will be remembered".

Fred was deeply devoted to our Divine Beloved Meher Baba, and I was aware of being in the presence of a true lover of God, who spoke softly and sincerely and gave from his heart.

Chapter Four - Called to India -'Three Incredible Weeks', 1954

Oh! I recall the time when near Thy dwelling was my stay.
Now I would my eyes were brightened by the dust of Thy doorway!

By Baba's grace Fred would not have to wait too long to see his Beloved again. In *Experiences* he recalled:

> During the early part of the year 1954, I was in the employ of a hospital in London and was called in for a check-up and detained for several months to recover from depletion. During this time, Will received a letter from Adi K Irani which he brought and read to me. The instructions were from Baba stating that I was to get well and attend the September 1954 meeting to be held in India. Will Backett was my travelling companion.

Only three men were invited from the United Kingdom – Charles Purdom, Will Backett, and Fred Marks and it would be radically life-changing for them all. Fred's early impressions of his journey to India were recorded in the *Awakener*[*1] as follows:

> August 1954, on board the S. S. Corfu
>
> This voyage from London to India at Baba's

invitation is my first visit to India. On leaving Southampton, I was pleasantly surprised when returning to my cabin to see a display of photographs of Baba and to have Mr. Dana Field from New York, who is also on his way to visit Baba, share the cabin with me.

During this brief interval, before arriving at Bombay, there are on this boat groups of nearly all the principle Western and Eastern religions which hope to take up various activities in different parts of the world. With infectious good humour, Dana says one has been reading the Bible to him and trying to 'convert him'. Such is the sincerity shown by some who in spiritual awakening turn feelingly towards others. Some have received Baba's Universal Message, and a few are showing still a deeper interest.

There is a general expectancy of a great happening. The end of the Age brings again the urge and longing for the One who will bring Redemption and save humanity from the abyss into which it has fallen. To find this One is to knowingly feel that there is nothing more to be desired. It is the end of the quest. His name today is MEHER BABA. He offers Himself to us. Baba is Light. He is the dynamo from which all spiritual activity proceeds. He is human and

Divine, His the Divine Will speeding through the channels of our being, Divine Love and Order. I go to be accepted by Him.

Fred's conviction is so beautifully and simply expressed and with such steadfast faith, we can feel his joyful anticipation of reunion with his Beloved Baba. The following text is a discreet account found in his papers and titled *Men's Sahavas Diaries*. I will refer to this and other sources to learn something of his visit. Of all sources, the diaries, sometimes written in the present tense, reflect most vividly the fragrance of those days.

The 'New' New Testament according to the Revelation recorded in the old New Testament of Him that was to come for the West and the East; King of Kings and Lord of Lords; the Messiah and Saviour; Messiah and Avatar to whom all religions belong, of which He is of none; that we might be found worthy of repentance. The Second Coming of Christ, from the Assembly of the Prophets is in our midst, to be proclaimed to them that dwell on earth and unto every nation:

Avatar Meher Baba – The Highest of the High! As He said in Andhra in March He had not 'come to raise the dead, but to make one dead to himself, to live for God, not to give sight to the blind, but to make people blind to the world in order to see God.'

The Journey to India

We arrived in Bombay and departed on Saturday, September 11th by hired coach. The company included Baba's followers from America, Australia, France, and Switzerland. We had our midday meal at Poona. Then we proceeded along the winding passes for almost 200 miles, mostly steep and mountainous. After passing through Ahmednagar, we arrive at the ashram on the hill. It is the first time Baba has admitted men at this retreat on the mount. The following record is of the Mass Darshan on Sunday, September 12, 1954.

When we leave the ashram for Ahmednagar in two cars, during the two-mile journey we pass continuous streams of people on foot, some in cars, and in bullock carts, beautifully neat and clean. Also, many people were arriving at Ahmednagar by train. Coming to the town we alight outside a long pandal, a flat-topped tent, erected in the park and decorated with flowers, red, white, and blue bunting, and Indian draperies. At one end is a raised dais and a large chair covered with loose tapestries.

Here comes Baba in a large blue car thronged on all sides by people. He proceeds to the dais. After several addresses by the mayor and other notabilities, the singers and the musicians begin playing and singing the bhajans or sacred songs. People start to pass Baba in single file to receive from His hands the sweets which have become priceless. The western followers have gained a place at the back of where Baba is sitting, and we are standing. Baba has got up from the chair and is sitting on the edge of the platform and it is almost impossible to see him. As the people pass, they garland him with ropes of fragrant flowers intertwined with jasmine or hyacinths and marigolds, which are continually being removed to be kept beside Him. Many also bring fruit as a sign of their devotion. Shouts and singing, and cries go up unceasingly.

"Avatar Meher Baba, Ki Jai"
(Hail Meher Baba the living Christ")

Basket upon basket of sweets arrive and are distributed by Baba to each recipient with graceful rapidity. Amidst the noise of the people, singing and bands playing, Baba continues through the hours of the Mass Darshan. Suddenly the announcers at the microphone must restore quiet for Baba is to give a message. Baba looks radiant, His eyes and face beaming with smiles; there is an atmosphere of fragrance and peacefulness; everyone has forgotten his or her troubles and Baba gives His message of beatification:

"If you were to ask me why I do not speak, I would say I am not silent, and that I speak more eloquently through gestures and the alphabet board. If you were to ask me why I do not talk, I would say mostly for three reasons. Firstly, I feel through all I am talking eternally; secondly, to relieve the boredom of talking incessantly through your forms, I keep silence in my personal physical form. And, thirdly, all talk is, in itself, idle talk. Lectures, messages, statements, discourses of any kind, spiritual or otherwise, imparted through utterances or writings, is just idle talk when not acted upon or lived up to.

If you ask when I will break my silence, I would say when I feel like uttering the only 'word' that was spoken in the beginning-less beginning, as that 'word' alone has worth. The time for the breaking of my outward silence to utter that 'word' is very near. When a person tells others be good, he conveys to his hearers the feeling that he is good, and they are not. When he says be brave, honest, and pure, he conveys to his hearers the feeling that the speaker is all that, whilst they are cowards, dishonest and unclean."

Baba later said:

"To love God in a practical way is to love our fellow beings.

If we feel for others as we feel for our own dear ones, we are loving God.

If instead of seeing faults in others, we look within ourselves, we are loving God.

If, instead of robbing others to help ourselves, we rob ourselves to help others, we are loving God.

If we suffer in the suffering of others, and feel happiness in the happiness of others, we are loving God.

If, instead of worrying over our own misfortunes, we think of ourselves to be more fortunate than many, many others, we are loving God.

If we endure our lot with patience and contentment, accepting it as his will, we are loving God.

If we understand and feel the greatest act of devotion and worship to God is not to hurt or harm any of his beings, we are loving God.

To love God as he ought to be loved, we must live for God and die for God, knowing that the goal of all life is to love God, and find him in our own self."

Again, Baba resumed His Darshan. The thousands of women with the little ones in their arms or by their sides, and old and young alike receive and offer their love. They try to touch or kiss his feet, but it is strictly forbidden, so closing the palms of their hands, they bow quickly and pass on. The eyes of some of the little ones remain focused on Baba as they pass before Him. There is much more in this ceremony than can be understood in the ordinary way. Baba offers and imparts to them His Divine Love. The hours pass by, and He continues serving the huge crowd. They are passing by Him at the speed of 45 per minute. The barrier is frequently having to be closed because of their eagerness to reach and to be near to Him.

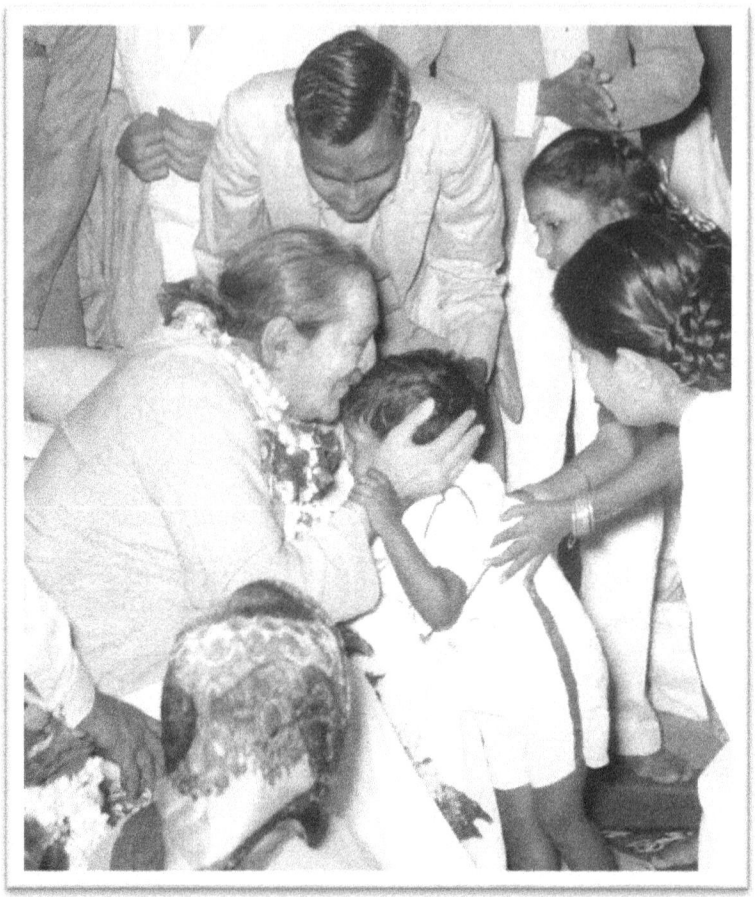

Baba has sent word for His western followers to return to the Ashram. It is noon day. They are told to return at 2:00 o'clock. Somehow, we manage to leave the dense throng and reach the car, but Baba continues. After the midday meal at the Retreat, we return to the Darshan. People are still flocking to the town, and as the party arrives at the pandal, we notice the sunbeams on Baba, as the breeze disturbs the hanging draperies overhead.

The photographers and filmmakers await every moment to seize any opportunity when a picture can be snapped. The shouts and singing and music continue. Voices are raised in union and the cry goes up 'Avatar Meher Baba, Ki Jai'. Two Saints have arrived who are very much respected by the people, and Baba gives them special embraces. He has invited them to sit beside him at his right. One is clothed in an under garment of white cotton muslin in shredded pieces and is holding a broken reed. As Baba embraces the other one, he removes from his head a piece of earthenware which at other times serves him as a utensil for eating purposes. Something indescribable emanates from these two souls. They are so reposeful and so calm. As I sit at the left side of Baba helping to support his back with my right arm and with the aid of cushion, officials and police continue to stem the crowds, but at intervals Baba swiftly breaks the continuity of the Darshan with messages.

Seven beggars, men advanced in years are brought to Baba, and with his sleeves rolled up, He performs the ceremony of bathing their feet. Then at lightning speed, having also disbanded Himself of his rose coloured half coat, again resumes the Darshan. For several hours I watched the hands of Baba, and the tiny, outstretched hands of the little ones, and the grown-up lovers as they were pressing, two abreast or single file, past Him. One tiny, outstretched hand was almost overlooked, but not by Baba, it received its portion of sweets.

By this time, it seems as though the barriers might collapse because of the swaying of the dense crowds of people, they are becoming so aggressive and possibly those controlling them might lose patience, but it is this sense of simple devotion so overpowering these poor people that Baba appeared to be enjoying, as though it was all in His plan.

Basket upon basket of sweets were arriving and I noticed how the white and beautiful hands are showing evident signs of becoming tender. Frequently the Indian disciples wipe his face and forehead of moisture with a kerchief as they lean over Him from behind. During these hours I shall always remember Baba's radiant smile, His enlightened face, the movements of His fingers and hands, a gesture of inward and outward grace or benediction to others, the offerings of flowers and the outstretched hands of those who came and went away because of their need of someone to love and be loved, it touched our hearts.

Baba asked for Purdom, and I turned around and caught the eye of Dana Field, and somehow, he got the message. Shortly after he was sitting near to Baba. (Will Backett was sought after by many Indian disciples who had previously met him in England or India, and when not seated near Baba, he was surrounded by admirers.)

The crowding out of the western disciples weakened and the opportunity offered itself for spontaneous service. Part of today's proceedings also included the feeding of 10,000 persons, apart from the Darshan which drew 35,000. Baba sat down with the multitude and partook of a morsel of food. Baba moves swiftly from one action to another, taking us by surprise. He is again vigorously distributing sweets with both hands at remarkable speed and continues towards the close of the day. The setting sun's rays beam upon His face through the pandal. It is 6:00 pm.

Suddenly He springs to His feet and after making signs with His fingers over the remaining pile of baskets of sweets, slips through the cordon made by the linked arms of his Indian disciples, and is next seen in a sitting posture with palms of both hands placed together. He has surmounted the top of the blue car and is being shaded from the far side by an umbrella held by a young Indian in western dress. Photographers are busy at remarkable speed as Baba moves slowly through the crowds towards the town, followed by the crowds crying 'Avatar Meher Baba Ki Jai!' Because of the insistence of the throng of people for Baba not to enter the car, He seats Himself upon it. The car gradually moves out of sight towards the town, the people following. In concluding, this eventful day reminded me of the sacred Christian song:

'At even e're the sun was set,
Oh, with what joy they went away.'*2

Truly it can be said, the Avatar awakens contemporary humanity to a realisation of its true spiritual nature, gives liberation to those who are ready, and quickens the life of the spirit in His time. For posterity is left the stimulating power of His divinely human example, the nobility of a life supremely lived, of a love unmixed with desire, of a power unused except for others, of a peace untroubled by ambition, of a knowledge undimmed by illusion. He has demonstrated the possibility of a divine life for all humanity.

Fred related in a talk with Irwin Luck in 1971[*3] that one day during the proceedings:

> Baba called me to Him for a private interview. This was on September 15th. This is what He imparted to me:

Early in 1951 I was in the employ of a hospital in London, but after a year or more I was called in for a 'check-up' and detained for several months to recover from depletion. During this time Will Backett paid a visit and read a letter informing me, Meher Baba had sent word stating I was to get well, and go to India and attend a special Meeting He was calling for men from the West. The Meeting took place on the 11° of September 1954 and I was subsequently present.
During this meeting Baba called me to Him for a private interview. This was on Sept 15. This is what He imparted to me,—
'I am the Ancient One. You know who I am.
As in the days of old I am drawing My fishermen. · · · · ·,'
When He made this statement, it is what is termed the bridging of the spiritual and physical between the Master and His devotee. I remained along with the other Western devotees on this visit for three weeks, and listened to discourses touching upon many phases of the aspirants spiritual progress. We were completely absorbent whilst He expounded the ways and methods of previous avatars in regard to their earthly mission to Humanity at the time of their particular epoch or cycle. He said He would return again in 700 years, when this phase of maternality will be at its climax.

"I am the Ancient One. You know who I am. As in the days of old, I am drawing My Fishermen."

When He made this statement, it is what is termed the bridging of the spiritual and physical between the

Master and His devotee. I remained along with the other western devotees on this visit for three weeks and listened to Discourses touching upon many phases of the aspirant's spiritual progress. We were completely absorbent whilst He expounded the ways and methods of previous Avatars regarding their earthly mission to humanity at the time of their epoch or cycle. He said He would return again in 700 years when this phase of materiality will be at its climax.

Purdom recounts an event later in the week:[*4]

On 20th September, Baba and His Mandali arranged a visit to Sakori, stopping en route at Rahuri, the location of Baba's Mast ashram. The purpose of the visit was to enable the pilgrims to pay their respects at the tomb shrine of the Perfect Master, Upasni Maharaj, who gave Baba Divine Knowledge and ultimately pronounced Him Avatar of the Age. Baba said:

"This old man (Upasni Maharaj) was God. I said at My last visit here that I would not stop again in Sakori. But I remembered that he had once said that visitors would come here from other lands to do devotion, and to fulfil this I had to come and bring you here. Now My work here is finished. After the meetings of the 29th and 30th, the following three months will be for My final work, to break My silence, to manifest, and then to die a violent death, all in quick succession. You should all bow down at Maharaj's tomb. I am the Ancient One. When he threw that stone at Me, I knew I was the Ancient One......"

After speaking, first Baba then all others bowed down in the room where Upasni Maharaj died. They all took food prepared by the nuns and visited other areas of the Ashram where songs were sung. Purdom continues:

> We left after a memorable day's experience. On the way back, Baba stopped and got out of His car to inquire about Fred Marks, who had hit his head on a low doorway and had been bound up by Baba.

It is hard to imagine Fred's experience of this day. He had been in India for just nine days with all that needed assimilating, and suddenly his Beloved Baba announces His imminent death. It is no wonder Fred forgot to duck under a low doorway, but how fortunate he was to receive such personal care from Beloved Baba on this profoundly unique day.

Returning to Fred's Men's Sahavas Diary, Fred recalled some stories:

23 September - Baba on Impressions, The Story of Satya Mang

Today Baba has explained how impressions or sanskaras are formed. Neither impression nor expression can free us from dualities. Impression or illusion is temporary passing phenomena - so long as it exists.

Something that is not, appears to be. This is illusion and this illusion then creates innumerable other petty illusions, and the experience of each illusion leaves behind the marks of experience in the form of impressions. When you are in bed you imagine and wake up. You see something, you reach for a stick and strike to kill it, but it was imagination, but it leaves an impression in your mind and one impression creates another impression.

Then Baba spoke to Will Donkin who came in, and Baba told him he would be responsible for us all being well, and as He spoke, Baba smiled in His usual way when He is in this mood. Don says he has a sore throat and John Bass and Lud Dimpfl are ill. Baba then spoke to us all and said, "Only if you love God as He should be loved can My work be accomplished."

Then He proceeded to tell us a story:

"At the Ashram in the early days I had a dear disciple who loved with his heart, but was a bit cracked in his head. Also, at this time a robber called Satya Mang was going about the country, and he was also using violence and murder. In time his gang terrorised people wherever he went. He exercised such influence that he was able to bribe the police, so that no one dared give any report against him because they feared becoming his victims. In his travels Satya Mang came to this village, Arangaon. I love the people here. It was one of my first Ashram's. Here I founded the dispensary, homes for the mentally afflicted, and leper hospitals. Wherever I go in the village the children come flocking to Me. There is poverty, mud huts, disease, but these people have love for Me. The children run out and shout "Baba, Baba, Ki Jai!"

This dear disciple, an Irani, was posted at the entrance to the Ashram on the Hill as the night watchman. It is the custom. It was known at this time Satya Mang was in the neighbourhood of the village at the bottom of the Hill. It happened that this disciple was posted on guard at the entrance of the Retreat. His usual habit was to throw up his arms and to shout, 'all's well', but one dark night while he was swinging the kerosene lamp he imagined through the shadows that he saw Satya Mang, so he immediately rushed into the Ashram and up the stone stairs, and bursting into the sleeping quarters, where the Mandali were all asleep, began to shout at the top of his voice 'Satya Mang is here'. Jumping up and down, he began to awaken the Mandali.

Some were very old women disciples. He worked himself into such a frenzy that they began to believe him. One old Mandali fainted. 'When I heard this story, Baba said, I thought it exceeded the Universal One I created ages ago'. So Bomanji, who was in charge, went to investigate. No sooner did he arrive, but he found a donkey jumping from one foothill to another! Then I sent for Satya Mang. He was staying in a small neighbouring town. Satya Mang said, 'I don't know Baba, get out' and abused the messenger. That night however, Satya Mang had a dream in which Baba was sitting on his chest, whereupon he left immediately to find Baba, arriving to find Him waiting with outstretched arms. He prostrated himself at Baba's feet and started weeping. Then I called him and made him sit quietly by my side. I want you from today to give up robbing and killing, and to disperse your gang, and for living come to me and I will supply you, I said. He promised. From that day Satya Mang dropped his old ways. In between stages Baba found him employment which provided just sufficient to meet the needs of himself, his
wife, and children.

When I went away to Persia, I left only one family here and I told Satya Mang to look after the place. The time came when I had plenty of money, though in the New Life I begged food, and made the Mandali beg from the poor. Satya Man went to the village begging for me. But during my absence Satya Mang relapsed to the point of attacking a very rich local man in a town a few miles distant who by profession was a moneylender. Satya Mang broke in and saw Baba standing there and submitted again, saying as he came to Baba in tears, "Baba, You have saved me!"

There were many miracles attributed to Me. Even now I receive letters that people see Baba in certain places. They say they have seen Me in My physical form, yet I tell them I have not yet performed a single miracle. It is their love and faith for Me. Baba's greatness, He continued, does not lie in performing miracles, but His greatness lies in suffering for the universe because He loves all.' (At another time Baba had explained to us the outstanding greatness of Jesus). When I break My silence, it will be My first and last miracle in this incarnation. If people tell you Baba has performed this or that miracle, let it go out the other ear."

Here Malcolm (*Schloss*) said, "Baba, will you

explain repression?" As Baba commenced to leave the room He replied to Malcolm, "You go and find out". We followed Baba outside the room, where He began to show us how to play marbles.

The Overflow Darshan at Ahmednagar - Sunday 26 September

Today we were met by Baba at Ahmednagar where he had been working several hours giving public Darshan, but His arrangements for the western followers that we should arrive at 3:00 pm was in consideration of us, because of the intense heat. Baba received each one of us separately and embraced us. The poor with their outbursts of love streamed up to the three-sided pandal with its flowers and green draperies, and devotees became immersed in the Divine Love of Baba. The daily duties and toils of householder or businessman, and the pastimes of the younger people, and the affections of the children all seem charged in this stream of mass devotion. There was a brief pause from Baba's playful moods when a little boy stood in front of Baba who smiled at him and removed his hat, and put it up on His own head, and then saluted the little fellow and in a soldierly fashion replaced the hat upon the little head. With others He garlanded them with flowers. At first upon being garlanded, little girls looked modestly astonished and then delighted. To behold the little ones was a joy, their hands linked in their mother's as they passed by, but their eyes glued on Baba.

Then there was a brief interval; the Saviour stood up and receded to the back of the pandal, on His face were visible signs of inmost suffering. He glanced downwards but His eyes seemed to have no part in the immediate physical surroundings. Again, resuming His activities to the constant stream of devotees, some old and infirm, whilst the outpouring of Divine Love is showered upon all.

Then Baba rose from the dais and slowly moved up the gravel pathway leading away. Someone was heard to say He was tired, but Baba replied He was not, and smilingly catching the officer in charge of the police by the hand, caught him up in a quick stride. The unexpected turned to humour as Baba gave him a benevolent pat on the back, the recipient lost his dignity and gave a broad smile and returned a friendly pat to Baba, such was the encouragement given to the officials responsible for mustering the thousands who came along that day. During this service He has stated to those seated on the pandal, 'no discourses here!'

(Baba was still working as we were instructed to return to the Retreat.)

The Saviour has called an eastern disciple to whom He is endeared. He is to sit at the feet of Baba and sing bhajans. As he takes up his position, looking up and glancing at Baba in shyness, his eyes then turn towards the Master's feet, and with a moment's effort the bhajan gains in tempo and praise, but within 5 minutes Baba said, 'I don't understand a word you are singing'. The devotee looked up to Baba's face perplexed, whereupon Baba smiled graciously and so being comforted, he ceased singing and had the good fortune to stroke Baba's feet. Both master and devotee shared the good humour and beamed with joy!

The Last Day of the Meeting, (During an Interlude), 30 September

We wait for Baba at the bottom of the hill, and the drive is lined on both sides by the crowd. He has sent a message He is taking us all up the hill. Baba appears followed by a huge crowd which is proclaiming the Saviour, 'Avatar Meher Baba, Ki Jai!'. He takes the lead up the hill and then sits under a tree near the entrance. The crowd of over 1000 is high spirited. Entering the grounds of the Retreat, He took the throng to the scene of His seclusion and explained that the white domed shrine is to be the last abode of His body. This was given to the followers in four languages.

We heard the story involving the boy, who on the instructions of Baba to the Mandali, during this year of seclusion in the small cabin, a flask of coffee should be sent to Him each day - this being His total sustenance for his physical needs. At the end of the seclusion the Mandali were asked to explain why only half a flask of coffee was sent to Him, and not in accordance with His order. They explained that the correct amount of coffee was dispatched to Baba in accordance with His instructions.

Then the little boy, whose daily task it was, and who comes from the neighbouring village, was called to Baba, who with a mixture of coaxes and endearments entreated him to be honest and explain about the coffee. Wearily he made a forthright confession:

"Baba," he said, "before I got to the top of the Hill, I felt tired!". To this story the crowd was very much amused. As Baba stood facing the huge crowd,

He sprung a question to the hearers: "When one offers another a drink from a vessel, what does it signify?"

The crowd of followers was quiet. Then Baba sprung the answer: "Prasad" He said, raising his voice, and the crowd laughed. Yes, it was that this little untouchable boy – so called - had unwittingly given Prasad to the Avatar.

Standing on the grey stone paving in front of the sleeping cabins, Baba explained the seclusion of an eastern disciple who for three years fasted on a glass of milk only each day. He was given strict orders that under no circumstances was he to speak. One day on waking he saw the head of a cobra which had raised itself above his own head. For three days he endured this. It was seen, and finally removed, by an attendant. Baba spoke highly of the endurance of this disciple.

We stood by the Tombshrine waiting for Baba to lead six of us in. Then we were directed three on either side, with Baba at the head. Here we bowed our heads in silence. One of the lady disciples has decorated the walls with a fresco. Outside the shrine Baba the Beloved has invited the westerners to sit on the ground beside Him to have a photograph taken. Then He slips away to the raised paving signalling us to join Him as he stands behind us for another photograph to be taken, permitting us to sit in front of Him.

Baba with the Western men, 1954 Meherabad Hill.

To conclude this account of Fred's first visit to India I want to share a brief anecdote that illustrates Fred's understanding of the significance of all that the Avatar touches when He comes as God Man. It also speaks volumes about his heart qualities. To quote Fred:

> The Prasad of Baba is God's Substance. During the time of the Westerners visit, (men only in India, September 1954), Baba gave each one an orange. The man from Greece threw away the orange peel. Another picked up the peel and put it in his pocket.

When he returned to England, he kept it. Apparently an American saw him pick up the peel. Fifteen years went by before the man from Greece laid claim to it when it was then sent directly to him.

How fortunate that man was that Fred paid attention both in the short and longer term, first by saving the orange peel, and then in returning it to him. Such was the tenderness of his heart for Baba and his fellow man.

To witness this extraordinary Darshan, the editor refers the reader to two beautiful DVDs. In the first *Meher Baba's Call,*[*5] we catch many glimpses of Fred standing head and shoulders above most others and witness his surrender to his Lord and Master as he falls to his knees to receive Baba's embrace. The second is the more recently released and delightfully narrated *Three Incredible Weeks with Meher Baba*[*6].

Baba directed Charles Purdom and Malcolm Schloss to keep diaries of the Darshan days. Extracts of these were first published in the *Awakener* which can be read online via the AMBPPCT Trust Library.[*7] Their combined diaries in their entirety are published in *Three Incredible Weeks with Meher Baba,*[*8]. Charles Purdom also recounts the events of that period in his comprehensive biography *The God-Man.*[*9]

***

Shortly before he passed, Lol Benbow, a longtime friend to Fred, shared these memories:

I was directed to Fred by two Baba lovers – Craig San Roque and Tanya Kennedy, who told me that "he is one for the Angels", or something very close to that and perfectly correct.

When I first visited Fred in his bedsit – it may have been the very first visit not sure - he showed me a shirt on a hanger on the wall. He said it was Baba's shirt bought at a men's outfitters on Piccadilly, now gone. *[The shirt is now in the London Baba Centre. Ed.]*. When I looked at this shirt, I saw a white shimmering light coming from it. Very beautiful. Then I sat across the table from him and saw Meher Baba instead of Fred. It is the only time I have seen Baba in colour. His face was large with lovely dark eyes and his cheeks were pink and His hair long and flowing like in the 1930s. His skin was delicate, and it made for a totally enchanting lifetime memory.

You may have seen a film where Baba is embracing men in a long queue. They come and embrace Him one after the other and then comes Fred Marks. Baba puts His hands to each side of his face and draws Fred's head down to His chest and places it against His heart. I may be mistaken but I regard this as exceptional – certainly no other man seen in the film was given this gift.

Another pointer is that there is a photo of Baba holding Fred's face close to His. Fred is bending down and Baba is seated. There are lots of people around them. One of them is Charles Purdom. Baba is looking deep into Fred's eyes. Fred told me that when He was released by Baba to stand up straight again, Baba turned to Charles Purdom and said, "this needs no words Charles".

I remember this clearly because after some years of contact with Fred, I found myself saying to him that my contact with him was not through words. He was full of wisdom and much more worldly wise than, at first, he seemed. We went to Nottingham once to take Baba's message there and he told me about a fault on my car. I was astonished because I am an amateur mechanic and did all the maintenance and repairs on the car. How did he know that, never having been underneath the vehicle? It turned out he was correct.

We went to Nottingham because he said they were his people, and that he had studied Fine Art and was a model for a mural in the Town Hall. He took me to see it – it was definitely Fred; you could tell by the size of his nose! A very good likeness.

He told me about an incident in London, outside St Paul's (I think). He was telling people about Baba and distributing leaflets. The vicar's wife came out and hung a notice over Baba's picture on the iron fence, advertising cups of tea or something. We both giggled. Fred was a very funny man, and musical. He took the trouble to learn the national anthem of every country and played them on the piano, though when I met him, he had forgotten many of them.

Meher Baba used to say of Fred "He is such a big man" and I think Fred always thought it was because of his size of over 6 ft. But one day he was at a gathering with many others around Baba, who asked, pointing to an Indian man at the far edge of the group, "how did you hear of Me?" and this man said, "from Mr Fred Marks of England." Yet Fred told me he had never met this man.

He was charming and diplomatic and explained to me that Baba had tasked him with taking His name all over England. He would go to Quaker meetings and bring Baba into his talks. He paid for cards to be printed for distribution at gatherings and we went together to meet Baba lovers in many places. One such meeting was with a lady who lived in Wales and had two sons, one of whom told many about Baba in New Zealand. That was Hilda Thorpe. When we visited her in Wales, she made us tea served in an old elegant- looking metal teapot. Fred picked it up and exclaimed it to be Cartier and made of silver! I think she said her brother gave it to her. I wonder if she polished it after that.

Fred had been an antique dealer near Marble Arch, I believe. Some of his clients were Royalty. Baba asked him to help Adi Junior in business and he told me Adi had exquisite taste and a very meticulous way of working. I ran into trouble with Adi, and Fred helped me to clear it up internally afterwards.

He was really very kind to me when I first contacted Baba followers in England in 1972. He advised me how to save money and when he started holding meetings in his flat, I was able to attend by finishing work at 3 p.m. and starting again the next day at 11 in the school where I was teaching. I drove to London for his Thursday evening meetings and was back in bed by 1 a.m. on Fridays.

Fred told me several times that he was present when Baba explained that USA and USSR, the then top powers, one would be devastated and the other permanently disabled. He (Fred) also said that he could never remember which was which!

Chapter Five - Christian Mysticism

If the sinner knew what bliss to me arises from the pardon of a sin,
He'd ever err intentionally, and with excuses, some new crime begin.

Whilst Fred may have taken his lead regarding Baba from Will and Mary during the early years, his journals reflect an early absorption concerning Christian Mysticism that pre-dated meeting Baba and became more developed following the '54 Darshan. Fred writes:

> In 1946 I wrote to Baba asking Him if Sufism and the Christian Faith were identical or in what way they differed. The reply was very short and implied that the approach was different, but both were identical in so far that the goal was the same. The letter pointed out that there was no fundamental difference. In Baba's reply He also stated that He was prepared to grant guidance and draw up a charter if one was, in all honesty, prepared to accept that role. This seemed to imply teaching and leadership under Baba's guidance, similar to the Sufi administration. Adi was accompanying Baba in the Himalayas at that time. Anyway, I got the impression that Christianity under a charter would function similarly to the Sufi movement under Baba's guidance.

108

In 1946 I wrote to Baba asking him if Sufism and the Christian faith were identical or in what way did they differ. The reply was very short and implied that the approach was different but both were identical insofar that the goal was the same. In Baba's reply He also stated that [He] was prepared to grant guidance and draw up a charter if one was [prepared] in all honesty to accept that role. This seemed to imply teaching and leadership, under Baba's guidance.

(The reply was belated because) Baba was accompanying Baba up in the Himalayas at that time. Anyway I got the impression that Christianity under a charter would function similar to the Sufi movement under Baba's guidance.

As will be seen in the volume 'God Speaks' Baba has placed the Vedantic, Mystic and Sufi approaches to God all on the same basis. The Christian approach is termed (Christian) Mysticism. The acceptance into the fabric of Christianity of the theories of evolution and re-incarnation as personal or individual approach means that Christian Mysticism is taking such a trend, and Baba out of His infinite skill and divine intervention is not neglecting many aspects of the aspirants' aspirations, individually and collectively or universally during this critical transition. However with Christian Mysticism re-oriented and which continues according to Baba's plan (Christian Mysticism was the last of the isms to be re-oriented or re-vivified) the aspirant is having to face the new advent in the spirit of adventure not as a crusade but as a something within his own being.

Towards this end and out of one's unbounded love to Baba, and love towards one's fellow human beings arises a new responsibility for visionary leadership.

Fred also recorded his thoughts on this topic following Baba's Final Declaration during the '54 Darshan. This was found in a loose-leaf format and was possibly written later after a period of reflection:

Baba defined to those present the purpose of His mission, what He intended to do, and the work for which those present had been called. Baba has explained in this age many truths to appease the intellectual approach to Truth. God cannot be approached nor even understood through the intellect alone. In His own way He will bring about a happy blending of the heart and mind of the aspirant. It was for this important phase of Meher Baba's work, that those called to be present at His Final Declaration were entrusted to be His instruments to carry out the channelling of the work.

It has already been stated that during Meher Baba's life, Ivy Duce was entrusted and appointed by Him as the head of the group under Baba's guidance for His reorientation of Sufism. I had received a letter in 1946 in which Baba had stated that Sufism and Christian Mysticism are fundamentally the same. The letter came from Adi Senior since Baba was on a visit to the Himalayas.

When Baba breaks His silence, from that one 'Word' AUM, the 'AMEN' of the Christian Mystic will resuscitate or re-vivify the language as a communication from God to Man and from Man to

God. The vital importance is that man will be enabled, through the Grace of the Perfect Master, to commune both inwardly in silence and outwardly by the same re-vivifying and vitalising force which will resuscitate the divine spirit in man.

Christian Mysticism is one of the four main principle 'isms' Meher Baba intends to reorient, revivify, or resuscitate within the spirit of man. It is already gradually yet slowly taking place. Meher Baba chose Christian Mysticism as the next in the order for His reorientation. When this happens, whereas today words have become meaningless, from that one 'Word' the AUM, all words will become meaningful.

Meher Baba spelt out on His alphabet board that He is approachable through any 'Ism' or no 'ism' at all. He is approachable by one and all.

When the Final Declaration was given out, those called were unable to understand at the time its deep significance. Baba called Don (Will Donkin) to stand on the platform and explain one aspect. Briefly, Don explained the aspect in question by giving a similitude. However, Baba spelt out on His alphabet board we were free to interpret it an any way we chose but it would be impossible for us to understand. It would take time before we really understood that which Baba was trying to convey to us. It is evident the real meaning had to unfold according to one's understanding.

Similarly, Buddha and Jesus veiled their statements, but even ordinary man is enabled to understand them at the time the spiritual manifestation gradually shines and purifies their hearts and intellect.

Christian Mysticism reoriented by Baba will be one of the Paths enabling the aspirants and initiates to enter the Path of the Beloved. Meher Baba 'imparted' to us that He has come to re-vivify or resuscitate the spirit of man so that once again it shall shine forth in its pristine glory. For the assignment and appointment of the leader Meher Baba chooses for 'channelling' Christian Mysticism is one whom in His own words is 'trustworthy and reliable'.

As will be seen in the volume *God Speaks,* Baba has placed the Vedantic, Mystic and Sufi approaches to God all on the same basis. The Christian approach is termed Christian Mysticism. The acceptance into the fabric of Christianity of the theories of evolution and re-incarnation as a personal or individual or universal approach means that Christian Mysticism is taking such a trend, and Baba out of His infinite skill and Divine intervention, is not neglecting any aspect of the aspirants' aspirations, individually and collectively, or universally, during this critical transition. It is my opinion however, with Christian Mysticism being re-oriented, and which continues according to Baba's plan, (Christian Mysticism was the last of the 'isms' to be reoriented or revivified), the aspirant is having to face the new advent in the spirit of adventure, not as a crusade, but as a searching within his own being.

Towards this end and out of one's unbounded love for Baba, and love towards one's fellow human beings, arises a new responsibility for visionary leadership. The nature of the development regarding this modern age is man's intellectual capacity and this must be offset and counter-balanced by a new approach to spirituality. First the aspirant should be convicted through the blending or fusion of the heart and mind, that Baba is the Christ – the God Man – in human form. The strength of the aspirant's conviction will be more and more stabilised as conviction and faith become the devotee's inner experience. At the same time intellect and reason will stand in abeyance.

'According to your faith will it be done unto you'[*1]

'If ye have faith, as a grain of mustard seed, ye shall say unto this mountain, remove hence to yonder and it shall remove'[*2]

Baba has come not to teach but to awaken, such awakening needs Baba's grace. Baba's grace alone will remove mountains (*of ignorance*).[*3]

Christ being without Sin had no need to be born for His incarnation as ordinary men are born. God is not to be understood. But it could be explained that God need not be circumscribed by His own laws and being above them is able to choose that best suited for His Incarnation during His life on earth. The conformity outwardly need not determine that inwardly. Is it important?

In a second notebook, sadly undated, Fred also writes the following:

Christian Mysticism is generally understood in the West to be something obscure, mysterious, occult, or esoteric. Such definitions could be considered and analysed ad infinitum. More to the point however, Christian Mysticism is experienced by self-surrender of the aspirant to the Master, whereby the spiritual apprehension is attained by direct communion with, and absorption in God. Truth may be apprehended directly by the soul without the intervention of the senses and intellect. Mysticism is not anti-intellectual, but it cannot be understood nor adequately explained through the intellect alone. Christian Mysticism is not a doctrine.

The questioning mind asks, 'then what is it?' It is spiritual experience. But the questioning mind is not the questing mind. The Master has crossed the path of the aspirant and the Love of the Master begins to search and transform the aspirant's heart. It then becomes the urge and the eternal quest of man in search of the Holy Grail and for which man has never lost hope – something he is yet to experience. When the goal is achieved, the Creator and the Created in essence become One, but in substance separate.

In Christian Mysticism the experience of the mystics might be described as a play of divinity in which the heart and will, mind and soul of the aspirant are surrendered to the Divine Will of the Master resulting in a mystical experience of Divine Love. The language of the heart is the language of the Kingdom of Heaven. In serving the heart, the mind becomes purified. The mundane and spiritual qualities are perceived in their relative values in respect of man and his divine nature. For instance, in the world of gross values, moral and human characteristics, the good and varying degrees of not 'good' qualities colour, or become, a man's character, but the true mystic sees far beyond such classifications, and since he is no longer bound by the pairs of opposites, such as 'good and evil', he radiates the Love of God. The true mystic has awareness that all are eventually destined to reach the goal.

The adventure and search for the 'Holy Grail' to drink of the cup of the elixir of life in eternity, engages the heart and mind of the aspirant in a restless participation to abandon the 'known' for the 'unknown', the unreal for the Real. The eternal quest of man to experience more and more of the Love of God that transforms the human heart and purifies the mind is typified by the cup of union.

Baba loves in the capacity of God to Man. To receive God's Love, Baba has come to give us Grace. Without His Grace we have not the capacity to receive God's love. Whereas Grace is a gift, Love is bestowed. Baba has stated that He can give more than one can ask for.

Embedded after the forgoing text, this paragraph seems like a prayer from Fred to Baba:

From earthly Self-forgetfulness, Awaken me to Baba, to heaven's Self-Awareness. Create in me a new heart and a new mind – to love and to serve and to be faithful in obedience.

He continues:

When asked what was meant by 'being spiritual', Baba replied: "To be spiritual means to be perfectly human. I have come to open wide the Gates of Heaven." – Meher Baba

Fred then records a verse from a hymn that would have been familiar to him from his youth and concludes his reflections with the statement that follows:

> There was none other good enough,
> To pay the price of sin.
> He alone, could unlock the Gates,
> Of Heaven and let us in.[*4]

Lovers of Meher Baba become the true mystics of God by containing the balance between the heart and the mind. The utterances of the mystic are spontaneous because the heart is single towards the Beloved and the mind and the heart for discrimination. The heart is the abode of the eloquence of silence, and yet it has its own language. Meher Baba looks upon the heart of the person.[*5]

***

Rosie Jackson remembers Fred:

Looking back on our personal contact with those who spent time with Meher Baba in physical form, I realise how little idea we had of the meaning of it, the privilege of it, to know those who had known Him. It seems to me rather like a tuning fork, those who were with Baba catching some of His vibration,

His light that then radiated through them towards us, transferring some quality of His ineffable presence. What a gift.

I met Fred Marks in 1981, when I was living in North London, soon after my first visit to India in the Christmas of 1980. I started attending the Thursday evening meetings held regularly in his weeny Putney home, basically one room with a tiny kitchen and bathroom, always packed with Baba lovers drawn like bees to his warm, quiet wisdom. Fred maintained that Thursdays were the best days for sacred gatherings, and that the ideal number for a group was 7 or thereabouts. Sometimes there were only 4 or 5 of us, sometimes rather more, the group flowing and ebbing around a core of regular attendees: Keith Ashton, Lol Benbow, Kathryn Coutu, Barbara Hayman, Michael Lakey, Steve Marions, Olive Pitt, Bill Pitt, myself, and sometimes Lisa Collins. When I moved to Bristol to teach in 1982, I continued to come when I could, sometimes racing up the M4 on the back of Lol's motorbike through the rain and darkness, keen to catch every possible moment of Fred's special presence.

The format of the meetings, as I recall them, was informal yet unvaried. Fred would offer some thoughts and reflections on an aspect of Baba's teachings, we would chat about them, make our own contributions, often in a meandering, inconclusive kind of way, then we would sing the English arti. Lol would play his guitar for a sing-along of Baba songs, before we proceeded to the serious business of cups of tea, snacks, and cakes, to which we'd brought our offerings, wheeled in on a trolley from the minute kitchen. It was all very modest, unpretentious, and very English.

Fred was invariably quietly spoken, mild mannered, courteous, impeccably polite. There is a scene in the film of the 'Three Incredible Weeks' where he falls to his knees before Baba and puts his face to Him, buries his face in His master, and I always saw him in this way, embodying perfect, graceful, and grateful surrender. Yet despite his mildness, there was running through Fred, like a lightning rod, his consummate faith and devotion to his Master. There was nothing soft about this. It was tangible, absolute, unconditional, so unequivocal as to be somewhat contagious, and we all drank of it thankfully. When Fred spoke of Baba, even his pronunciation of the name sounded holy, full of love, and the tiny room was filled with a sense of the sacred and numinous. Perhaps his Christian background partly accounted for this, but Fred seemed to me firmly in a line of Christian mystics, able to both access and in some way transmit the essence of the Avatar's wondrous reality as both God and man.

On one occasion in 1982, Lol Benbow and I took Fred to a viewing of Richard Attenborough's newly released film *Gandhi* at a large London cinema. I remember walking down to the front to buy ice creams (those were the days when ice creams were sold from usherettes in the interval), and when I turned back to look at Fred, a huge halo of light seemed to emanate from where he was sitting, making me wonder what work Baba might be doing through him in such a crowd. On another occasion, when I made some remark about the very difficult relationship I had with my mother, Fred said gently but firmly, 'You must be grateful to your mother. She is the one who gave you the body through which you have come to hear of the Avatar. We must all be grateful to our parents for this.' And he was unstintingly encouraging. One day, when I shared that my birthday fell on the same day as Shakespeare's birthday, April 23rd, Fred turned to me with not a scrap of irony – he did fun, but not irony – and said 'Rosie, you are more important than Shakespeare. You are with Meher Baba.' And when I feel invisible or unrecognised, I remind myself of that.

Fred did not strike me as a worldly man; in the world but not of it, his enduring connection to Meher Baba a love and devotion as fine and beautiful as a spider's thread, as strong and obdurate as steel.

Chapter Six – Reunion in London, 1956

Welcome the morn that brings my loved one home!
Thanks that the Partner of my cares has come.

Only two years passed before Fred had the opportunity to meet his Beloved again when Baba made what would be His final visit to London in July, stopping off en route to New York. Baba's disciples could not know that in December of that eventful year, Baba would experience His second critical car accident in Satara which would result in untold suffering, and that His mobility would be severely impaired for the rest of His life.

When Fred was reunited with Beloved Baba for the first time since those Three Incredible Weeks in 1954, it is recorded that:

> Fred Marks told Baba that his love for Him had increased, and Baba embraced him, delighted by the news.[*1]

This is what Fred remembered when speaking to Irwin Luck many years later:

> In 1956 Baba came to London for what was to

be His last UK visit. He stayed at the Hotel Rubens. I was one present to meet Him. Now, there was a Committee Meeting on the ground floor, and there were several Baba lovers waiting to see Him. Baba was engaged with important people about the future of the Committee, (*for Meher Baba's Universal Spiritual League*) while the lovers were waiting in the lounge. At the same time there was a Garden Party going on at Buckingham Palace, which is opposite at the eastern entrance of the Hotel Rubens.

The secretary came to me, and she said in front of Baba, (Baba was present and myself and the secretary), and she said, "I want you to wear this blue ribbon for people coming so that you can direct them to Baba". This took me by surprise because I always feel that where Baba is, there is no need for any sort of show. However, Baba saw that I was reluctant, and I caught his eye and at that very moment, it was conveyed to me, 'do it, but do it for Me' and I did it, because I feel Baba can convey truth. Whatever He wants, He can convey in a manner known only to Himself. It can be experienced in infinite ways.

('Fred Marks stood by the door with a royal blue sash across his chest like a steward.')[*2].

On the first day Baba was dealing with the Committee agenda for the future months, and for some reason I'd written a paper which somehow went to Baba, and He came to me. We were in a bedroom upstairs, three of us. I remember Anne Powell, one of his greatest lovers known as Welsh Anne, whom He called Welsh Anne, and Edmund Purdom and there was another Baba lover there, we sat on the bed.

Baba came and He walked past the bed, and he went to the window and the Guards, one of the Footguards Band, was playing and Baba snapped his fingers to the tune of the Band, and I wondered what that conveyed to Him, but it was very significant because everything that Baba does has some infinite significance for the future, and for the present.

('At one point during the morning the Royal Guards fife and drums corps was passing on its way to the Garden Party at the Palace. Delia ran to get Baba who, smiling, had a peek from Max's window. While observing and snapping his fingers to the music, Baba reminded Fred Marks of Lord Krishna.')[*3].

The paper that I was speaking about was given the heading *Meher Baba - the Lord of Mercy*[*4], because when Baba was in his younger days in India, someone gave him a pamphlet, and on this pamphlet it spoke of the Buddha when he would come again as the Maitreya, which means 'the Lord of Mercy' and this was a reminder to Baba. And He granted that concession, and that paper has been printed, and Baba said it was to be sent out over the earth to all His Baba lovers at that time.

Since then, the young people have asked for this paper in England, and they take it back to the United States where the young people have not met Baba, but they seem to feel something personal in this message of His. It is very personal and compassionate.

An evening reception was held in one of the largest hotel rooms described by the Hopkinsons as follows:-

Against a background of purple hangings, on a

settee placed in the centre of one wall, covered with glowing satin and velvet cushions and flanked with massive flower displays, Baba looked truly regal. Some two hundred followers came up one by one to be greeted. It was a moving scene, and for most of those present it formed their last visual memory of their Master, since he never came back again to Britain.[*5].

For this reason, it seems important to include this message that Baba gave directly to His early British lovers:

"One who hears the music of God in his heart, such wonderful music, for it is the original music, loses his bodily consciousness and sees God everywhere. God is within everyone. He is in all of us - Infinite, All Powerful. The helplessness that you feel now, here as you are in the body, is an illusion although God is so omnipotent. Why is that? It is illusion. It is the veil between you and God. The veil of what? The veil is the veil of ignorance. Once you come to know that the body is not real and this body is not you, then that veil of ignorance is lifted. When you are indeed asleep, the body is there although you are not.

The body breathes and yet you are not aware of its breathing when you are asleep; then you may dream you eat, or in the dream you go to the pictures. It is not the body that dreams. It must be something that dreams; it must be YOU. Suppose this body has its legs cut off; you are in no way less conscious, nor do you feel that there is any curtailment in your own existence. You are still you and your consciousness is not curtailed. Mind understands, yet the veil of illusion is not lifted because of the veil of ignorance which you still have.

Once you see God within you, you get that conviction of God. There is no more doubt. Then there is the experience of infinite bliss. I give my blessing to you all. If those who love me will just for one minute, as now, be silent in their minds just before they go to bed and think of Me and picture Me in the silence of their minds, and do that regularly, then this veil of ignorance that they have will disappear and this bliss that I speak of, and which all long for, they shall experience." - Meher Baba[*6].

We do not know if Fred intended to follow Baba swiftly to America, or whether this profound Discourse put wings on his feet, but we learnt from a letter sent years later to David

128

Fenster, editor of *Lord Meher,* that Fred indeed must have swiftly packed his bags and followed Baba's party, scheduled to travel via New York to Myrtle Beach. It is the only archival evidence we have found to date to substantiate his attendance. Clearly Fred was destined to continue his sojourn with his Lord.

Baba departing London Airport 1956, Fred looking on lovingly.

***

Phil Simpson writes of Fred:

Based on our short acquaintance, what I'd like to say is that Fred once said to me: 'When Baba is not exalted, He suffers.'

Sometimes when I visited him and spoke about mundane matters, my feeling was that I was making Fred suffer by distracting him from exalting Baba.

***

Scott McKeig from the US shared his memories of meeting Fred a number of times in London:

I met Fred Marks in the Baba Centre in London in 1970 when Bob Brown and I were on our way to India. We'd both been to the Great Darshan, and at that time people were so overwhelmed by that experience that we weren't thinking of going back to India. But someone named Tom Fortson arrived in Myrtle Beach, and we sat at the little table in the kitchen with him and we heard that he'd been to Meherabad and Meherazad, and he was just beaming. Bob and I basically looked at each other and said, 'excuse us', and the next morning we went to New York, found things to sell, and took Icelandic airlines to London. That's when I met Fred at the Baba Centre, over a tea. I was immediately struck. He was on a similar wavelength, and Bob was also struck. We met Mary Parry also that day.

We had a couple days preparing to go to India and we wondered how we could see Fred Marks again, as we didn't have an address for him. We had to go down to the Indian Embassy to get our instant Indian visa, which was possible in those days. It was noon and very busy. We jumped on a double-decker bus - and you know they have that sideways seat as you go in the door - well there was Fred Marks, sitting next to two empty seats, smiling! We had just enough time to make an appointment, and then our stop came. We met with Fred in his little basement digs and we were both very impressed. We didn't go back together again, but each of us did go through London and make a special point of spending time with Fred again.

Fred was quite mystical; the Christian mystic flavour was very strong in him. One time I went and there was an older man there talking, and Fred motioned me to be quiet. This man was talking about flying saucers or something. When he left Fred said, 'well, I met him at Speaker's Corner. He was actually talking about the planes of consciousness!'

The last time I went, it may have been three times, his knees pained him so terribly, but he was in a nicer place. He gave us a play that he'd written. I decided to put it on for Baba's birthday, in Berkeley in 1972. It was a short play, and we did our best. It included a climactic moment when the script says 5 minutes of silence. Now, when you're giving a play and then there's 5 minutes of silence, it really makes an impression!

Chapter Seven – American Sahavas, July 1956 and May 1958

My home is in the Beloved's Street, how fair a spot is it!
No man of sense in all the world would such a dwelling quit.

July, 1956

Fred left few clues about his first visit to the Meher Center in 1956, but most likely he travelled there directly from London. On 24th July, those people whom Baba had met in New York, and who were accompanying Him to Myrtle Beach, departed. Over the following days more than 150 guests came, many Meeting Baba for the first time. For some, like Kitty Davy, it was the first reunion with Baba since the accident in 1952, and photos of the time clearly reflect her complete joy. It was an intimate time where He gave personal interviews to close ones in the Lagoon Cabin, and group talks in the Barn. Though Elizabeth's car was on hand, Baba sometimes walked between the cabins, the Barn and beach surrounded by His lovers, perhaps to reassure them of His recovery since His accident. Baba remarked that, of all places, the Center was where He felt most comfortable. There are some lovely accounts of this Sahavas in *Lord Meher*, including Baba's explanation of St. Francis being raised to

Perfection by the Sufi Prophet Khwaja Khizr, thus becoming the only Perfect Master in the West in His time. We can imagine, because of Fred's earlier vision of St. Francis, that this would have held particular significance for him.

Fred would no doubt have enjoyed meeting friends from the '54 Darshan, including Darwin Shaw and Dana Field. A new acquaintance, who was to figure some years later in his life, was Carrie Ben Shammai from Israel who had only recently met Baba in New York. She had fallen so completely for Him that she felt drawn to follow Him to Myrtle Beach to spend more time with Him. She tells her Baba story in a two-part film by Martin Cook which can be found on YouTube. [*1]

Returning later to Israel she, like Fred, felt impelled to spread Baba's messages there. In the video she describes how the task of running regular groups and keeping up with correspondence in subsequent years was overwhelming and so, years later, she approached Fred for help. Fred was very willing to go at his own expense, and letters held in the MEM Archives in India show that Fred had written back and forth both to Carrie and to Adi seeking Baba's advice, trying to arrange for this work to happen. In one from Adi dated 4th December 1964, Adi writes:

Baba approves of your going to Israel for His work there. He sends His love to you and wants you to convey His Love and Blessings to the people of Israel and especially to those who love Baba.

Fred states in his reply to Adi that he could only obtain one week off work, and Carrie says in the video that she had been hopeful for months of help from Fred. In the last letter which the Trust holds relating to this exchange with Fred, dated 1ˢᵗ October 1964, she writes:

> It had been our wish for you to come and work here and Baba did not only mind but found you most suitable for this. But it had not been His wish, He just let us be, provided time and money should be available. So, we cannot force our way against Baba's Will which obviously has not come yet for you to help us here in our Baba work. It will be in Baba's time and not in our limited illusory one. Needless to say, again and again how happy we should be when time and circumstances in His Wish only might arrive for this. This might be at any moment if it will be His Wish. But up to date, time is not right for it yet.

> Be happy in His Only Will.

> Love from us here in Him and from Carrie.

So, it was not meant to be; but seemingly one outcome of the '56 American Sahavas was that Baba was establishing a network of His Western lovers, who would each, like Fred, serve in their own way and in their own countries, gathering new disciples to unfold the next wave of His New Humanity.

May, 1958

Two years passed and once again Fred, along with other British Baba lovers including Delia DeLeon, Mary Parry, Charles Purdom, Hilda Thorpe and her son, travelled to Myrtle Beach to meet Baba again. Fred had been busy distributing *Meher Baba - Lord of Mercy,* Baba leaflets and cards. This second Myrtle Beach Sahavas would be very different from the '56 gathering, as in December of that year Baba had experienced his second motor accident in Satara and, with other injuries, had broken His right hip, leaving Him thereafter in constant pain. Charles Purdom recounting the Sahavas in *The God-Man*[*2] wrote that prior to travelling to the West, Baba had sent the following potent message to His lovers:

> My suffering is daily becoming more intense, and my health is daily getting worse, but my physical body continues to bear the burden. Despite it I shall hold the Sahavas. I expect from you a deep understanding of My imposed suffering, begotten of compassion and love for mankind….

I may give you more, much more than you expect – or maybe nothing, and that nothing may prove to be everything. So, I say, come with open hearts to receive much or nothing from your Divine Beloved. Come prepared to receive not so much of My words but of My Silence.'

Travelling with Baba were Dr. W. Donkin, Adi K. Irani, Eruch Jessawala and Nariman Dadachanji, all of whom Fred knew from his previous times with Baba. Two hundred and twenty-five persons came, including those from England, France, Switzerland, Israel, Mexico and naturally from the U.S. Many families brought their children, and that contributed to a lively atmosphere. Aside from Purdom's detailed account in his biography, there are wonderful accounts in the *Awakener* - Special Sahavas Issue, 1958[*3].

Mary Parry's name appears together with Fred's in the Guest Register in Baba's House. Mary recounted to Martin Cook that they were mistakenly presumed to be a couple, having arrived at the same time. Indeed, they were close friends in Baba's work, and both were responsible for distributing many thousands of Baba leaflets in subsequent years.

Mary Parry, from Bradford, who also recognised
Baba's Divinity in the early '30s

Perhaps the most potent outcome of Fred's time in Myrtle Beach is evidenced in Part Two of this book - his *Experiences* manuscript, which distils much that Fred imbibed. Baba gave more than twenty Discourses and it seemed to all gathered that He was working intensely, and He also allowed those present to witness something of His suffering. He asked for His message, 'My Wish', to be read out three times. We know this impacted significantly upon Fred as he refers to it in his subsequent writings, and those who knew him testify to his living faithfully to those directives.

58

The New-new Testament
The Gospel of Love — of Meher Baba.

—— My Wish ——

The lover has to keep the wish of the Beloved. My wish for My lovers is as follows:

1. Do not shirk your responsibilities.

2. Attend faithfully to your worldly duties, but always keep at the back of your mind that all this is Baba's.

3. When you feel happy think 'Baba wants me to be happy'. When you suffer think 'Baba wants me to suffer'.

4. Be resigned to every situation and think honestly and sincerely, 'Baba has placed me in this situation'.

5. With the understanding that Baba is in everyone, try to help and serve others.

6. I say with My Divine Authority to each and all that whosoever takes My Name at the time of breathing his last, comes to Me; so do not forget to remember Me in your last moments. Unless you start to remember Me from now onwards it will be difficult to remember Me when your end approaches. You should start practising

from now on. Even if you take My name only once every day you will not forget to remember Me in your dying moments.

After an interval Baba had His wish read again. This was at Myrtle Beach, Saturday 24ᵗʰ May, 1955.
The discourse was read a third time.
Hehe Baba made known His Wish for his lovers and for those of the present Humanity who come and believe in him through his lovers, both in the present and in the generation to come.
Baba's wish is to enable us to become spiritual beneficiaries according to His divine will. This will is unequivocally universal, One and inseparable.

When Baba gave His discourse on the 'Split Ego' and the 'False 'I', he used Fred as a point of reference saying:

"Here is Fred Marks from London. He is actually God; he is omnipotent, omniscient, omnipresent. But God in Marks says, 'I am helpless, I am here, I do not know everything.' The God in Marks says, 'I am a Man'. The God in Mrs. de Blasio says, 'I am a Woman'. But God is neither man nor woman. This distinction is due to imagination".*⁴

No doubt this gave Fred cause to ponder his 'God state' for many years to come, and indeed he explores this theme in the passage entitled 'Knowing', in *Experiences*.

In short, despite having said He may give nothing, Baba was most generous in His giving, including hosting a Birthday Party for 40 children whose lives were changed forever by the experience. Dee Dee Eaton, one of those fortunate children whom Baba embraced that day, recalled her mother saying that Fred pushed her on a swing rigged on a nearby tree. It is delightful to think of Fred, who was generally rather shy, enjoying such a playful moment at the Center. Many of those who attended remember the Sahavas as joyful and free, despite moments when Baba was clearly preoccupied with His world work, as can be seen in some images taken at that time.

On the beach, (from left to right) Fred, then Charles Purdom, Dorothea (Dottie) Foot, and Adi K Irani almost out of shot.

(Image by kind permission of Sufism Reoriented)

Regardless of the absence of a journal of his experiences there, we have several letters either to or from Fred that reference the '58 Sahavas. One comes from Baba's sister Mani, apparently in response to a letter of gratitude that Fred must have sent to Baba on his return. It is dated 11th July 1958.

Dear Fred,

I can't agree with you about your not finding words to fit, your few lines seemed to bring the essence of His Beloved Sahavas more than many another letter. Perhaps because it is the language I love and understand best too - to hear God speak through nature, the song of the birds, the trees, the crickets, the roses. They were part of this Sahavas also and expressed their love in special overflow. And the delightful way the animal kingdom shared too - what with the alligators that inspired the performance to make him smile; and I hear one morning a turtle just walked into the barn to say hello to his Creator - someone carried the lucky fellow over to Baba and Baba touched him, and they say turtles are slow on the uptake!

Delia spoke of another 'C' meeting in July, and I do hope Adi was well to be able to attend it. We read in the papers that this was the wettest June in England for 50 years so dear Dara will have to wait till next summer to see the natural beauty of that country as we endearingly remember. Or perhaps it may still be this year. I had Freni's loving letter two days ago and will be writing them soon. They always speak with much love of you dear ones who are truly a family to them.

'Because of His Word, all words will have meaning' - a beautiful truth, beautifully expressed. Baba said, "Tell Fred he is right, and He sends you His love."

Yesterday we planted a white champa tree in our garden in commemoration of this 10th July. It is about 3 feet high and already in flower and the sky blessed it, and all trees and fields with the much prayed for rain....

With much love as always dear Fred, in Baba,

Mani

Thereafter, more practical correspondence flowed from one lover to another on various aspects of their encounters in Baba. One was addressed to Dana Field, an American disciple who had become a firm friend in Baba since the '54 Darshan.

It is dated 29th September 1958. This is of greater significance since it references Fred having a personal meeting with Baba, presumably in the Lagoon Cabin. I infer from it that Baba directly encouraged Fred to hold meetings in His name in London and then, through the offer of financial help from one Mrs. A. D., this was made possible for Fred to actualise. As we know, because of the nature of his work, Fred had a modest income. I include the relevant transcript of the letter for the reader to draw their own conclusions:

Dear Dana,

Now with regard to dear Mrs D, I will explain. When at Myrtle Beach, Beloved, on one occasion, called me to sit down near Him. He made a certain remark to me, and it is because of that I am accepting A's spontaneous offer to meet expenses regarding meetings to spread Baba's message. In regard to this, a detailed account will be sent. The future meeting is costing 30 shillings including cost of hall or room, and advertising. I shall be attending them every three weeks or once a month in various parts of London. Should I need the cooperation of the Committee, (not money), their help will be asked for.

Tomorrow they are meeting to discuss ways I have

suggested to them by which they can help, because I have made it clear to them, I shall not be accepting any money in any way for expenses, or remittance for books et cetera. I have told Will *[Backett]* I am accepting A's offer. She should send a cheque by getting Bank in Arizona to transfer by airmail in New York, the dollars to England. I hope she is well again.

It seems also a long time since I saw Irene Conybeare. Please give her my love. Tomorrow I shall write to A.D. When you write, will you correspond to the address as written here above. In moving about, I have had to discard unnecessary items, but your shirts have been a boon in service to me.

In Baba's love and service to you,

Brotherly love. Fred Marks

So, clearly, friendships deepened and Fred established a growing network of contacts who would facilitate his on-going work. Not surprisingly things didn't always go smoothly! Fred was to receive a rather excoriating letter from Adi, sanctioned by Baba, when at one time he acted on his own impulse rather than a direct order. I include the entire text as it reveals so many elements of the Master-disciple relationship, and the intimacy Baba maintained with his 'world workers'. This was dated 3rd May 1960 and is written in Adi Senior's hand:

My dear Fred,

I read your letter of April 23rd on April 29th. The book left with Will Backett for disposal has created a misunderstanding. The sale of the book has nothing to do with Baba needing money. In fact, Baba does not need money and does not accept money as gifts. The book in question was an antique left behind by one of Baba's old late lovers which Meherjee gave Don Stevens, to get a better price in the West. Don Stevens gave it to Will Backett through Allan, thinking Will was most suitable for the job. I hope you received my today's cable which I reproduce here:

'Baba does not accept gifts. Inform all concerned. Adi.'

Now you have to bear in mind seriously one thing, unless Baba sends you direct instructions, you should not, and must not act upon anything you hear from anyone. Such acts invariably create wrong movements. Baba did not at all like the idea of your having sent the money as suggested in your above letter received. Baba knows how much you love him and also knows that it is out of this very sincere love and consideration you sent the money. But this has created a mess. Wrong conclusion drawn from information not coming as direct instructions from Baba, going from one ear to another of Baba's lovers multiply misunderstanding and create greater mess.

Now Baba says you should not worry for what is already done. Baba pardons you for this. Baba wants you further to be careful of any such future situation and not act upon anything and especially money matters, unless directly instructed by Baba. Baba wishes me again to tell you that you should not worry about what is past. You should be careful for the future. You, Will and Mary are Baba's close ones and Baba knows all this was the outcome of your deep and silent love for Him.

Baba sends His dear Love and Blessings to you.

Yours brotherly,

Adi Senior

In November 1961 there is a letter from Will Backett regarding a special meeting Fred was proposing to mark the anniversary of the US Sahavas. In an extract from it Will says:

Many thanks for your suggestion for a special meeting in the first half of this month, with music reminiscent of Baba's Presence at Myrtle Beach, which would help to recreate the experience of your days there with Him. On 16th Dec. the C'tee has arranged the annual Xmas party and next year Delia, who was at Myrtle Beach, will be rota Chairman. So why not suggest it to her for I don't think she has settled the subject for each monthly meeting?'

Will clearly felt they could not manage a second meeting in the winter months, but it shows Fred's enthusiasm for keeping Baba meetings in constant focus. Evidently Will, Mary and Fred worked as a team, and I quote in its entirety an especially poignant letter from the Backetts which so beautifully reveals how Baba was at the very core of their truly humble lives, where every spare pound was utilised on their Baba work.

Dec 17, 1961

Dear Fred,

We are quite overwhelmed when opening your tiny envelope last evening together, to find such a big, big present from you again, especially after you had already given double the amount to the printing of the 'Observer' correspondence. However, this very morning the opportunity has come to use some of it for direct work connected with Beloved Baba which we know you will regard as a happy privilege, indeed as we do, and we are sure other opportunities will also come to utilise the rest similarly. On the other hand, you are surely in the same position,[*5] which makes us doubly grateful for your further loving cooperation yesterday. We look forward to seeing you in the New Year when we shall have a few 'Observer' letters to show you of great interest - though not the response in numbers we had hoped. May Baba's blessings unite us ever in His Service that is 'Perfect Freedom'.

Ever, your old friend, Will

And then, penned below and along the side margin, a continuation from Mary:

Dear Mark,[*6]

We both feel very much your kind thought in sending us such a generous Christmas gift, and the charming little card. I'm rather a kid still and love the sparkles on Christmas cards! It is especially good of you to send the five pounds as you had helped so greatly over the Observer letters - there is no joy like that of doing Baba's work - I know you will feel His love with our heartfelt thanks added. I had been so wishing for a pound or two to do one or two little things for His work. It is horrid to be too old to work, but He gives us all our different chances to take part. Will says you spoke of coming over, so do let us know when you are free. I was so glad to hear that your landlady was able to go to the party and meet Ann.

With love and all good wishes for a very Happy Christmas and New Year in Baba's Love

Mary

Regarding the two American Sahavas, Sufism Reoriented recently, (*2023*), uploaded a high quality film of '*Meher Baba's Sahavas in America, 1956, 1958*' to YouTube. It contains the most beautiful footage of Baba moving so very gracefully around the Centre in 1956, before His second auto accident. This contrasts with His need to be carried in a sedan chair by various lovers during His 1958 visit. One fortunate lover who had this opportunity was indeed 'dear Fred', as Baba called him, who can be seen holding the left rear corner of the chair behind Raphael Rudd. How blessed was he!

***

Rob Barton, a British Baba lover residing in Myrtle Beach, shared memories of Fred with the Editor in January 2022:

Rob remembered walking through Hyde Park and coming across Fred Marks at 'Speaker's Corner'.[*7] He was wearing a Baba badge so Rob, who already knew about Baba, approached him and they got talking for quite some time. Later Rob confessed to Fred that he was visiting London and had nowhere to stay. Fred immediately reassured him that he could help and told him about the Baba premises at Eccleston Square where apparently a key was left under a stone outside. Fred only remarked that he must not 'advertise this favour'. Rob duly found the flat and enjoyed a good night's sleep, letting himself out the following morning.

Fred had told Rob that he felt he was bound to tell people about Meher Baba, and he would carry with him a popular coloured photograph of Baba, which bore the quote "True happiness lies in making other people happy". Rob observed that Fred had painted out the words. Rob and I wondered whether, in his humility, Fred felt it was an outcome he could not personally guarantee.

***

Anne Barker, who lives in Asheville, remembers Fred thus:

1978 was my first trip to the Meher Center; I travelled down from Indiana. I saw that Fred Marks was going to speak, and it was his first time back at the Center since his visit with Meher Baba in 1958. As he was introduced, he very slowly stood up and very, very slowly walked to the stage and then slowly walked over to the seat. Then he simply sat there with his head bowed, not saying a word for about two or three minutes, and the audience began to be uneasy and turn and stare at one another and make faces such as 'what the heck's going on'. Then finally he began to talk. I was simply mesmerised. There was so much humility in his comments and such an incredible depth of love for Meher Baba that I was simply blown away by him. Now, other people were not. Some thought his talk a little tame, and one person who was in charge of the library wanted to throw away the audio of his talk, but I was like, 'no don't do that, it was a wonderful talk'. After that I was simply in love with him, and I would have dreams about going to London, getting an apartment in the same building with my little daughter, and I would dream of taking care of him.

I'm still just fascinated by him, and I also recall in the book, *The Three Incredible Weeks*, that one of the participants said all of us were just regular guys, except of course for Fred Marks and Darwin Shaw who are Saints. It was even recognised by those people that these two were very special beings.

Chapter Eight - Filis Frederick

Of myself I can do nothing, but Your praise declare,
I am your servant cradled in your care.

Filis was a significant contact for Fred, especially throughout the '50s, though they remained in touch for decades. Correspondence in Fred's archive reveals that Will and Mary Backett connected them and he had already been reading *The Awakener Magazine,* which she began publishing in 1953. (It was later simply referred to as the *Awakener*.) Both Filis and Fred recognised Baba as their Master long before they met Him face to face in the same year, 1952 - Filis in Myrtle Beach, and Fred barely a month later in London. After the 1954 Darshan, Filis had requested some accounts of Baba's Discourses for the magazine, and amongst other sahavasees had approached Fred. He wrote as follows:

> First, I want to thank you all for the *Awakener*, it has helped me very much. During the Discourses, although each day I sat next to Malcolm Schloss, who suggested we might share in the records, I did not have the opportunity to do so; what I was not able to record fully were the Discourses on the 'Planes'. Mary Backett has asked me if I would send you my records of the Discourses by Baba on:

* Impressions or Illusions, (which includes the story of Satya Mang the robber).

* The Last Day, September 30th, 1954 (An interlude with Baba as he relates the story of the untouchable boy and the coffee.)

*A record of the Mass Darshan, September 12th, and overflow September 26th, 1954

As soon as you have taken what material you require from these records will you kindly dispatch them back to me, (16 pages).

Ever united in Baba's love to all of you,

Fred Marks[*1]

Fred and Filis enjoyed a spiritual dialogue unfolding in the 'Real time' of Baba's presence on earth. I include an example as follows, written by Fred on April 20th, 1955.

Dearest Miss Filis Frederick,

I am very glad to hear from you and have noted contents of your letter. Dana Field says he has received help through me. I do not know, but in the mere loving of one another we perhaps do receive help.

In your letter touching upon the subject of Baba's Last Circular April 1st, 1955, Satara, I have copied a letter which others have received here. There is nothing new, but it may clarify a little.

The Last Circular from Baba seems to confirm the previous one with profound additional knowledge concerning God as Reality. Here perhaps reference to the 'Hierarchy of the Saints' will clarify. The article is by Dr. Abdul Ghani Munsiff, page 427, May 1940, Meher Baba Journal. The theme of the abovementioned article was embodied in symbology in a picture Baba was holding whilst He sat on His divan just before the rendering of the prayers in the Great Prayer Hall, September 29th, 1954.

> According to the Sufis, at the crucial moment the Qutub (avatar or messiah) steps out of the Universe and another takes his place. As this might be understood better the avatar - physical effects the physical Universe. This might be understood as the Spiritual push which takes place at that moment. In Christian terms it is referred to as the 'atonement' (at-one-ment)

After the meeting, the same day He instructed this picture to be one of others to be photographed in colour. According to the Sufi's, at 'the crucial moment' the Qutub, (Avatar or Messiah), steps out of the Universe, another takes His place. As this might be understood better, the Avatar physically affects the physical Universe. This might be understood as 'the spiritual push' which takes place at that moment. In

Christian terms it is referred to as the 'Atonement' (at-one-ment).

It seems throughout the whole of the transitional stages of the Avatar, from Personal to Impersonal, His unbounded Love and Infinite Mercy remain unbroken with humanity. This also is recorded in the Bible:

'His mercy endureth forever and is from everlasting to everlasting'*2.

The lower levels affecting humanity's illusory phases, animate and inanimate, and the illusory laws identified with national, international, social, moral, and so forth become effective according to their time processes. These are effects from Him and hence the illusory process begins again. The Old Testament of the Bible records the choice of the people between a prophet or a king. They chose a king. This was conceded and established. This might be understood as a partial manifestation of law in illusion. You mentioned, however, destruction of sanskaras, or 3/4 of humanity. 'The Removal or Dispersion of Sanskaras' (Discourses Volume 1 and 11 by Baba) are explained by Baba as you know.

All man's vehicles, gross and finer, and surroundings

are waylaid by the shock. Hence in the past and the present, Prophets warn and prepare humanity through the age-long call to Repentance, prior to the upheaval, as spiritual preparation for them to receive the Messianic or Apostolic Message (Ekadashi) of Redemption which proclaims the Avatar or Messiah - both before and after His world Manifestation on Earth. Along with the upheaval, with the destruction of law in illusion, is the phenomenon of manifestations on higher spiritual levels (also illusions), but which not only sustain but also strengthen the faith of the spiritually prepared ones. The effect of shock may destroy the vehicle of sanskaras or cause a psychic upheaval. In the individual this is coordinated and brought into harmony through the Grace of the Master.

AND NOW TO THE BELOVED WHO SAYS ONLY LOVE FOR GOD WILL COUNT NOW.

Fred Marks

It seems almost certain that Fred finally met Filis face to face in 1956 in Myrtle Beach. They were definitely there in 1958 as the following letter was sent soon after Fred's return to the UK. It concerns payments relating to lockets purchased by Delia DeLeon and Mary Parry while in the US. It opens with this touching paragraph:

> I hope this finds you well and happy. My thoughts of you are always surcharged with Baba's (*M.Beach*) overflow. It is so sufficient and invigorating to dwell in thought on our last meeting at Myrtle Beach. *[The remaining detail of the letter concerned payments. Ed]*

Loving Regards in Baba to you dear Filis,

Fred

The tone of this last letter is so much more familiar, even intimate, following their Myrtle Beach encounters. Inevitably the correspondence continued, with Fred sending articles that piqued his interest and which he believed she might wish to share with her readers. The following is just such an example:-

The Indian Cricket Team

Baba personally gave the following message to the Indian Cricket Team before they left to play a Test Match in the UK, in 1959. They were also each given a copy of *Life at Its Best*[*3]

"When you take the field, if you play as eleven men as one heart, each enjoying the excellence of performance in another player as he would in himself, whether that player is on your side or the opposing team, and so eliminating feelings of jealousy, anger, and pride, which so often mar sport, you will not only be entertaining the spectators but be demonstrating the real spirit of sportsmanship. True sportsmanship is concentrated ability enlivened by sincere appreciation of the performance of others, and when this is manifested, everyone both players and spectators, receive spiritual upliftment as well as good entertainment. Some of you are allrounders. I am a spiritual allrounder. I feel equally at home with saints, yogis, philosophers, and cricketers, as well as with sinners and scoundrels. I give you My Blessing that in all your actions you should show the spirit of love. - Meher Baba"

Fred enclosed the foregoing message in this letter to Filis dated 16th July 1959 offering his own commentary on ensuing outcomes while the team were actually in England. It reads:

Dear Filis,

The enclosed message was given by Baba to the India team when each member received a copy of *Life at its Best* from Baba, before leaving for England. The English Captain of the cricket team had received a copy of the message by way of an introduction through an English National newspaper, which had placed the biographical sketch of Meher Baba in its reference library for retention against possible use in the future. The English Captain accordingly received what he calls that excellent book, *Life at its Best* - Meher Baba.

The rules of cricket have changed little since the game was first played. There is however one exception, the speed of fast bowling, which may be the outcome of a symptom of the present age, as against the original art of simple slow bowling sped along the pitch with a graceful twist also giving a delightful misjudgement of speed for the batsman in playing off the ball.

Just prior to the first Test Match at Nottingham, the English team which had indulged in violent fast bowling, the brilliant sunshine became obscured, a thunderclap and a downpour of rain followed, and the pitch was saturated. Probably the misleading news items inculcating excitement caused the losing team also to apply the swift bowling instead of the staid, slow, and composed tactics. Nonetheless probably, the losers from the spiritual point of view were actually the winners.

Once at Meherabad in 1954 September, Baba suddenly took up the bat at the ping pong table and engaged Lud Dimpfl. Baba served the ball twice to Lud. It sped like a flash of lightning across the table, Lud lost both strokes. Baba laid down the bat and immediately vanished. An onlooker, one of Baba's lovers, still conscious of the lightning swipe of Baba, took up the game with Lud and won the first stroke and then he forgot Baba and lost the second stroke to Lud. Probably both the English and India teams forgot to remember Baba's advice.

Lovingly yours in Baba,

Fred Marks

In April 1961, at the suggestion of Will and Mary, Fred sent Filis the pamphlet *Meher Baba - Lord of Mercy*[*4] that he had prepared and gifted to Baba when he met Him in London in 1956, and that Baba had sanctioned. He hoped Filis would print it in *The Awakener*. Fred had already circulated it widely as a typed document, but it had not been published per se.

1 Balmuir gardens,
Putney. S.W.15.
London.

16 April 1961.

Dear Filis,

I hope you are well. It seems a happy phase you are now going through. The above district in London is a very prosperous one and Baba's instructions are that I was to remain here until His instructions gave further orders. In the poor district I found the people more attentive and easy to approach.

The enclosed article 'Avatar Meher Baba - Lord of Unbounded mercy' is being sent to you for printing in the 'Awakener.'

I had decided to re-draft it, and had begun when Will Backett wrote me suggesting he would have it put before the Committee here with a view to it being printed in pamphlet form, so I considered it time to do something about it, although a type-written copy has been widely distributed here.

I have decided to leave out the dates, as they are not important in regard to the substance of the article, so I leave it with you.

Lastly Will has written me this morning to say he feels sure you will be pleased to use it for the 'Awakener.'

With Love, as Ever in Baba.
From Fred Marks.

Evidently, as mentioned in a later letter to Fred and Ella Winterfeld, Filis had instead replied requesting Fred write something (new), 'especially for them', but Fred was trying hard to fulfil Baba's directive to publish the text that He had personally sanctioned far and wide, so Fred wrote again to Filis on the same subject August 10th stating:

> The article which I sent you has the indelible stamp of BABA on it, and when Baba accepted it, at that time, I understood through Mary Backett that He was most emphatic that it should not be altered. The few words that were inserted by me in the present copy you have, is to render it more easy for one's understanding. Will Backett asks me to remind you that the article was only sent to a few, but over a wide area, and Baba instructed this at the time immediately after it was written, as you will see, it has His blessing.....

And again, dear Fred followed up with a letter on 12th November saying:

> I have not heard from you, but I have to write to you again in regard to the article *Avatar Meher Baba - Lord of Unbound Mercy.* This is rather urgent, however if you will post the Article on to me, I shall

be pleased because it has to go to India, and this means that I shall have to receive it <u>within </u>the next fortnight so as to enable the person going to have possession of it.

As if to soften his somewhat complaining tone Fred added:

You may, if you wish, take a copy of it.

My Dearest Love to you in Baba,

Fred Marks.

Since Philip Creager, who resides in Myrtle Beach was able to kindly share his own personal copy, clearly it was eventually printed, so Fred's persistence was rewarded.

The content of his pamphlet is timeless. Reading it now, we gain direct insight into Fred's lived experience when he says:

'To meet Meher Baba, to feel or even know of Him can be the end of all human questing. In Him there can be nothing more to be desired. Neither is there anything which is outside His being.'

164

MEHER BABA

Lord of Mercy

Meher Baba

Lord of Mercy

MESSIAH OF THE AGE

When from the depths of his heart man cries to be delivered from the upheavals and psychic disturbances of his mind, and the unredeemed loneliness of his heart which bring about crisis, and where human power is powerless he becomes the recipient of the unbounded mercy of GOD.

Thus, man becomes consciously sustained whilst the descending grace of God, and the divine co-operation between God and man brings to him divine co-ordination and here is bestowed the gift of abiding peace, beyond understanding.

Where words fail to convey to another being the depth of human experience, it becomes real salvation when the Divine Call, surcharged with the unfathomable force of Love brings forth an awakening and awareness so deep and transcendent.

The Gospel message of Christ becomes living truth when heart and mind consciousness become transformed. The whole being is immersed in an ocean of divine Love.

Through stages of spiritual awareness comes the certainty that the ONE who is here, Incarnate and in our very midst, and whose name is known to-day as MEHER BABA,—throughout East and West, brings to fulfillment the hopes of all humanity in all that has been declared and written by the prophets in the holy scriptures.

MEHER BABA the Avatar (MESSIAH) whose name means Compassionate Father brings forth life into Existence and directs it to its goal.

To meet Meher Baba, to feel or even know of Him can be the end of all human questing. In him there can be nothing more to be desired. Neither is there anything which is outside His Being.

" Every being is an open book for the infinite searchlight of His omnipresent consciousness. He is, because of His union with the infinite endowed with unlimited power. God's perfection is revealed when He manifests Himself as man.

" The conscious descent of God into the limited form of man is known as the Messiah and this again is a state of perfection.

" If there is lack of happiness, beauty or goodness in those by whom the master is surrounded, these very things become for him the opportunity to shower his divine love upon them and to redeem them from the state of spiritual and material poverty.

166

"So, his everyday responses to his worldly environment become expressions of dynamic and creative divinity which spreads itself and spiritualises everything in which he puts his mind.

To the simple lovers of God who approach Him, Baba gives direct messages, and to meet the needs of all he has given explanations through profound and long discourses.

He says : —

"Come to Me. Come All unto Me. Come to Me
with your impurities. Hide nothing—from Me.
Bring me all your weaknesses, give them all to
Me, only 'GIVE.' I will make you free, unbound
and happy. Serve Him Who serves the whole
universe; obey Him Who Commands the whole creation;
Love Him Who is Love Itself; follow Him in every walk of
life. I feel everyone of you to be Mine and I want
everyone of you to make Me yours, as you are already
eternally Mine. There is nothing which is beyond Me,
yet I am and can always be captured with love. For the
Infinite Love I bear for one and all I come as the
Avatar (Messiah) to be judged time and again by humanity
in its ignorance, in order to help man to distinguish the
Real from the false.

When My Universal Religion of Love is on the verge of
fading into insignificance, I come to breathe ' life ' into
it, and do away with the farce of dogmas that defile it
in the name of ' religions,' and stifle it with ceremony
and rituals.

To affirm religious faiths, to establish societies or
to hold conferences will never bring about the feeling
of Unity and One-ness in the life of mankind.
Unity in the midst of diversity can be made to be felt.
only by touching the very core of the heart !
That is the work for which I have come.

" I HAVE COME TO SOW THE SEED OF LOVE IN YOUR
HEARTS, SO THAT IN SPITE OF ALL SUPERFICIAL
DIVERSITY, WHICH YOUR LIFE IN ILLUSION MUST
EXPERIENCE AND ENDURE, THE FEELING OF ONE-
NESS THROUGH LOVE, IS BROUGHT ABOUT AMONGST
ALL THE NATIONS, CREEDS, SECTS AND
SOCIAL DISTINCTIONS OF THE WORLD.

IN ORDER TO BRING THIS ABOUT, I AM PREPARING
TO BREAK MY SILENCE.

IT WILL NOT BE TO FILL YOUR EARS WITH
SPIRITUAL LECTURES. I SHALL SPEAK ONLY *ONE
WORD* AND THIS 'WORD' WILL PENETRATE THE
HEARTS OF ALL MEN, AND EVEN MAKE THE SINNER
FEEL THAT HE IS MEANT TO BE A SAINT, WHILE THE
SAINT WILL KNOW THAT GOD DWELLS IN THE
SINNER AS MUCH AS HE IS IN HIMSELF.

I AM THE DIVINE BELOVED WHO LOVES YOU
MORE THAN YOU CAN EVER LOVE YOURSELF!"

Conceded by Avatar Meher Baba,

London, Aug. 1954
FRED MARKS

The foregoing pages, *Meher Baba – Lord of Mercy*, is the text that Fred had presented to Baba for His approval during the 1956 Sahavas in London. Fred distributed it worldwide over subsequent decades, thus finally fulfilling what he believed was Baba's wish.

It would be remiss not to conclude this chapter by acknowledging the unique and precious gift *The Awakener Magazine* has been to the collective history of Beloved Baba's life. It is so rich in content concerning His direct Messages, and in presenting first-hand accounts by those who met Him. This remains Filis' enduring and priceless legacy.

The entire collection is now available to read on-line at *www.theawakenermagazine.org*.

Fred reading a copy of Awakener.

***

Philip Creager, who resides in Myrtle Beach and for many years hosted the *Discourses* meetings at the Meher Center after Darwin Shaw's passing, remembers Fred from a personal diary entry dated Feb 7th, 1980:

I visited Fred Marks today and we talked for nearly six hours, (mostly he talked, I am glad to say). A truly wonderful soul, not to mention a unique personality; independent. He told me several things, (experiences) specifying, "this is just between you and me." One thing was when he gave blood despite poor health and they evidently took too much and the nurse got him tea (!) to revive him, which it did. He saw, inwardly, St Francis give the nurse the tea to give to him; he's only told two other people this.

Another thing, in what is now the Meherabad Hill Library, he was alone with Baba and He told him, "I am the Ancient One. You know who I am. I have come for the fishermen".

This was in 1954 and Fred had known that God was on earth since God spoke to him (inwardly) at 9 am, June 15th, 1933 - but now he knew he was meeting that God, Himself. (He had met Baba before the Library visit). It was an indescribable experience he says. Baba's work with Fred entails telling people about Baba. These are people he meets on the street, in parks, on buses, etc. They include some pretty 'messed-up' people. He lives very, very, simply. He is very gentle, very sensitive, and has a certain innocence. He reminds me of Darwin *[Shaw - Ed.]* in a number of ways.

Fred thought Olive Pitt was 'advanced', and recounted standing at Speaker's Corner with the poster of Baba that states: 'Real Happiness Lies in Making Others Happy', but the words were painted out.[*5]

Chapter Nine - Begin the Beguine

Heaven's sovereign Lord knows all your secrets,
He can your every hair and vein describe.

It is almost inevitable that within very few decades, *Begin the Beguine*[*1] may become one of the best known and most loved songs of all time, if not for eternity. For lovers of Beloved Baba, it already holds a place of deep affection in their hearts, and on hearing the opening bars over a radio, in a store or restaurant, we can be instantly transported to Baba's Samadhi, where it was played seven times during His Entombment. We may reflect on His Avatarhood and His Beloved Mehera, who experienced the agony of separation after Baba dropped His physical form. Indeed, it is so charged with resonance that most Baba lovers stop in their tracks the moment they hear the melody.

Many have stories to tell of a particular time in their lives when the song lifted them from some point of despair, or sealed their conviction that Baba was indeed present in a moment of personal significance. Knowing that dear Fred Marks played his part in finding the Cole Porter recording that Baba longed for, it behoves me to relate his story.

Fred records:

Mani sent word to England that a gramophone recording of a song called *Begin the Beguine*, *(a recording by the singer Leslie (Hutch) Hutchinson)*, was required for Baba. It was the only one in existence of this particular recording, the Mandali already had a version of the song in jazz. Baba does not care for jazz. The song was written and composed by Cole Porter who was soldiering in the U.S. Army. It was being sung by Leslie Hutchinson in London cabaret night clubs. He also played at the piano. It was during the war. Cole Porter songs were usually romantic with a strong appeal.

Because it was war time everyone in one way or another was suffering through separation but drawn closer through love ties. Cole Porter sustained severe loss of leg, and 'Hutch', as he was then called was a young man – lonely and somewhat aloof from his patrons. The record, *Begin the Beguine,* had some hidden appeal at the time, a sort of mystical and latent quality. Baba was asked the meaning of the words and He explained. For Baba lovers the meaning of the words has a bearing and significance regarding His mission to Humanity.

I turned over stacks of records wherever they were

to be found in second hand shops, or in private collections. Eventually I came across the record.'

Fred wrote to Mani of his find, and a reply came dated 1st May 1961:

Dear Fred,

Your letter of Springtime brought with it the fragrance of your love for Baba, and the news that you have found an original rendering of *Begin the Beguine* recorded on His Master's Voice disc, is as exciting as that of discovering a rare orchid in a basket of artificial flowers. I cannot imagine how you did it, and yet on the other hand I am not surprised dear Fred that you did; and shall be most happy to play it to Baba from you. Yes, there is the possibility of someone coming to India in the near future - though I believe it is not in June but in August. The person concerned is Najoo, a Baba lover from here who went for about a year's study to the USA in the Government's plan for Health Administration (India) and she will be returning (according to her letter just received) possibly in August - via London where she hopes to stop for a few days. She will be the best person to bring it over, and I find from experience that the best way to pack it is first between corrugated cardboard and then between thick stiff pieces of cardboard or light stiff plywood. (Packed in soft wool and flannel as Adi did, is not a good support).

I hope this finds you in good health and cheer. Our news will be coming later on in the family letter. The goldmohur trees are aflame with blossom and we're soon expecting the thunderstorms of May.

In Baba's love that is always with you, very lovingly, Mani.

I am also writing Delia and shall mention about this too. Love Mani*2

It transpired that Najoo Kotwal did indeed carry the record to India (7th September 1961), and so it reached Meherazad intact. After Fred passed away, Bill Pitt who was a close friend of Fred's, found in his room a greetings card from Mani to Fred with a floral image on the front. It read:

Baba's dear, dear Fred,

It is 4:00 o'clock in the afternoon and Baba has gone over to the Mandali after just having heard the record of *Begin the Beguine* that reached us yesterday. It is a very beautiful rendering of this song, and Beloved Baba is most happy with it. He liked it so much that he had it played twice, and I can see it shall be played often. It sang the love from your heart to Him, and Baba is happy you searched for it, and found it. It is the end of our united search because for years we have been trying to get a suitable rendering of this favourite song of Baba's and a number of them came to us, (including two that Dr. Kenmore brought with him), but it was not what was wanted. Yours is the perfect one and has made our Perfect One happy. Najoo too brought it with such care, nursing it like a baby. And how wonderfully you had packed it Fred, (one wood piece is already fixed on my typing stool), and I mustn't forget to mention that Baba looked at the sheet on which the words of the song had been typed, and passed His finger all round, across the raised handmade border of leaves you had designed, and the heart beneath.

We will not be seeing Najoo yet, for Baba's seclusion continues stricter than ever for the rest of the year, but she handed the things to Adi Snr. who had been to Bombay on the 5th to attend a wedding of a dear Baba boy in Bombay. (Dadachanji's brother Dara). I chose this particular card, floral, to carry this special message dear Fred, knowing your touch and love for flowers. Here the jasmine is in season, and all the bowers of jasmine vine are thickly studded with the milky stars. We missed the goldmohur blossoming but the white champa are perennially fascinating whether in bloom, or leaf, or bare. I hope you are keeping in good health, and I know you are keeping happy in Baba's love, for Baba is always with you, and that is the biggest and every reason to be happy.

With very loving greetings and wishes to you from all Meherazadians dear Fred, and with love Mani.

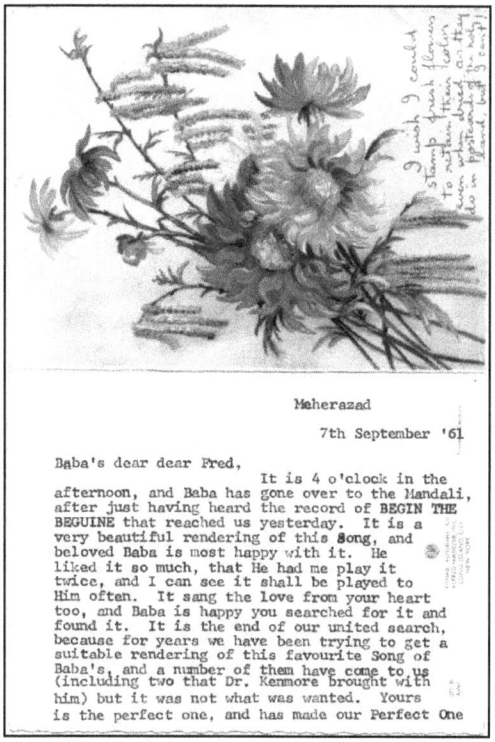

Maherazad

7th September '61

Baba's dear dear Fred,

It is 4 o'clock in the afternoon, and Baba has gone over to the Mandali, after just having heard the record of BEGIN THE BEGUINE that reached us yesterday. It is a very beautiful rendering of this Song, and beloved Baba is most happy with it. He liked it so much, that He had me play it twice, and I can see it shall be played to Him often. It sang the love from your heart too, and Baba is happy you searched for it and found it. It is the end of our united search, because for years we have been trying to get a suitable rendering of this favourite Song of Baba's, and a number of them have come to us (including two that Dr. Kenmore brought with him) but it was not what was wanted. Yours is the perfect one, and has made our Perfect One

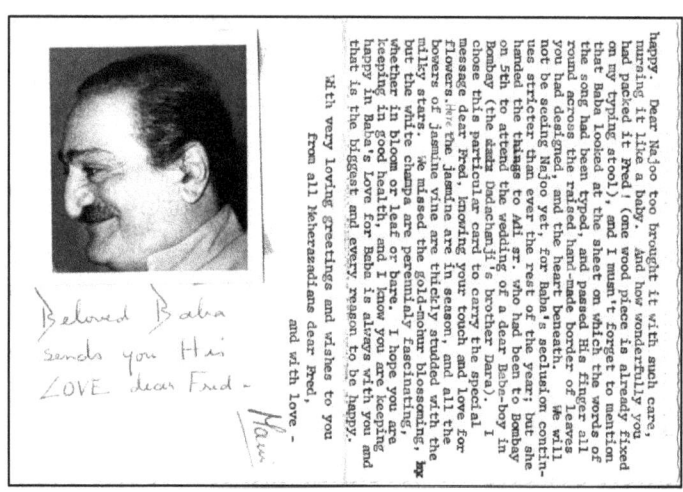

happy. Dear Najoo too brought it with such care, nursing it like a baby. And how wonderfully you had packed it Fred! (one wood piece is already fixed on my typing stool), and I musn't forget to mention that Baba looked at the sheet on which the words of the song had been typed, and passed His finger all round across the raised hand-made border of leaves you had designed, and the heart beneath. We will not be seeing Najoo yet, for Baba's seclusion continues stricter than ever for the rest of the year; but she handed the things to Adi sr. who had been to Bombay on 5th to attend the wedding of a dear Baba-boy in Bombay (the Baba Dadachanji's brother Dara). I chose this particular card to carry the special message dear Fred, knowing your touch and love for flowers, where the Jasmine are in season, and all the bowers of Jasmine vine are thickly studded with the white champa and the gold-mohr blossoming, but the whole champa are perennially fascinating, whether in bloom or leaf or bare. I hope you are keeping in good health, and I know you are keeping happy in Baba's Love for Baba is always with you and that is the biggest and every reason to be happy.

with very loving greetings and wishes to you from all Meherazadians dear Fred, and with Love –

Mani –

Beloved Baba sends you His LOVE dear Fred –

Another small rose-embellished card from Mani, dated 23rd September 1961, was amongst the correspondence found by

Keith Miles, which thanked Fred for sending a 'Sapphire Needle' for playing their discs:

> Dear Fred,
>
> How dear of you to have sent the sapphire needle - it will be wonderfully useful on our dear old gramophone for all the records. Apart from its undoubted excellence in clarity of tone, it has saved the problem of acquiring good steel needles and keeping them in good condition. Your undivided love has reached the Inseparable One and He sends you more of His love dear Fred that yours may grow and become ever more undivided. It includes the love from all at Meherazad. Am enclosing another little card our Warren has just made at my request using the 'silence' picture he had used for the bookmarks.
>
> With much love in Baba, Mani'

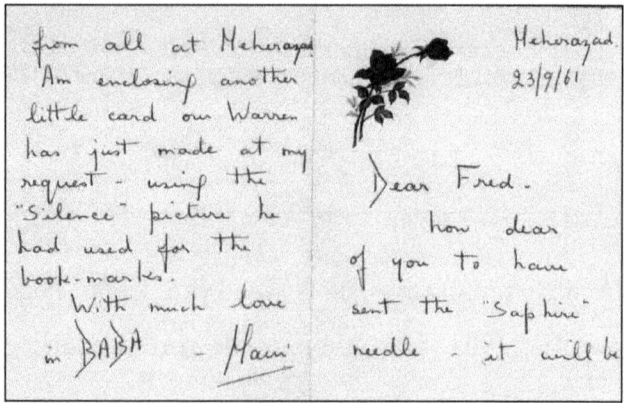

> wonderfully useful on our dear old
> gramophone, for all the records. Apart
> from its undoubted excellence in clarity
> of tone it has saved the problem of
> acquiring good steel needles + keeping
> them in good condition.
>
> Your undivided love has reached
> The Inseparable One - and He sends
> you more of His Love dear Fred that
> yours may grow + become ever more
> undivided. It includes the love

In November 1984 Fred was asked to give a talk at the London Centre and he chose the theme *Begin the Beguine*. The following is a transcript of that talk:[*3]

The hazards which are being exerted in every direction in the world today to resuscitate, or do away with the present order of things, has brought men to a state of perplexity and bewilderment, so I take my role of work in Baba's cause not as a teacher or a philosopher, but more directly as a witness, and quickly passed on from things as they are, to what they might be for those of us who are Baba aspirants and lovers in Baba, who have to be in the world without getting caught up in it.

The subject of my talk today is centred around Baba's favourite song *Begin the Beguine*. In short, the history of the origin of the song is simply incidental. In 1930s when the *Beguine* was first sung in London, the song did not give much interest to people probably because it was enveloped in obscurity. Baba was however in England at that time. Cole Porter, the composer of the *Beguine,* produced another song in 1936 called *Spread it Abroad.* Leslie Hutchinson, known as 'Hutch', singer and pianist, took them up with much enthusiasm. Artists all over the world clamoured to sing the *Beguine* but Hutch had the exclusive rights. He was a much-loved personality and respected the material entrusted to him and was careful to interpret it in the spirit in which it was created. Cole Porter composed songs on the nature of human love which seemed to be inspired by the Divine. The *Beguine* however transcends the whole range of human love, and the composer becomes the visionary of the Divine. It can be assumed Baba crossed the paths of both singer and composer, and either one or the other or both, were agents for Baba, who stated the *Beguine* meant a great deal spiritually.

It was in August 1961 when Baba sent word to England for a search to be made for this original recording of the *Beguine.* It seemed almost impossible to come by, like searching for the Holy Grail. Eventually it was found, and Mani wrote, 'it is the end of our united search, it is the perfect one, and it has made our Perfect One happy.'

Begin the Beguine.

When they begin the Beguine
It brings back the sound of music so tender
It brings back a night of tropical splendour
It brings back a memory ever green.

I'm with you once more under the stars
And down by the shore an orchestra's playing,
And even the palms seem to be swaying
When they begin the Beguine.

To live it again is past all endeavour,
Except when that tune clutches my heart,
And there we are, swearing to love for ever,
And promising never, never to part.

What moments divine, what rapture serene,
Till clouds came along to disperse the joys we
                                    had tasted
And now when I hear people curse the chance
                                    that was wasted
I know too well what they mean;

So don't let them begin the Beguine,
Let the love that was once a fire remain an ember;
Let it sleep like the dead desire I only, remember
When they begin the Beguine.

Oh yes, let them begin the Beguine,
Till the stars that were there before return above you,
Till you whisper to me once more, Darling I love you! "
And we suddenly know what heaven we're in,
When they begin the Beguine.—When they begin the
                                    Beguine

The *Beguine* is the story of the soul's journey from the beyond God to the end of illusion, when the soul knows 'I am God'. We all know that in the beginning there was a ripple over the divine ocean, and that that ripple caused waves, and drops appeared. Those drops which were in fact ocean did not know they had forgotten this still calm ocean, and knew themselves only as drops, and each drop said, 'who am I?'

The *Beguine* describes the splendour of God who knows everything and sees into the way each drop will act. He knows each drop will have many experiences and will forget Him, even though they are Him. He tells us in the *Beguine* how at times He cannot bear to recall how these drops suffer until he says one drop begins to look at itself and thinks, who am I? And then again clutches his heart, and the drop thinks about God and the clouds again appear and once again the drop forgets. Again and again, these drops appear to remember God, and again and again they forget as illusion forces them back to their illusion.

Baba once said that He was so fed up with the world that He had a mind to send it all back to stone, and I think that feeling is perfectly described in the penultimate verse of the *Beguine* – 'let the love that was once a fire remain an ember'. And then he says 'no, let them begin the Beguine'. I'll charm them, those who really love, I'll make them adore Me. They shall become my lovers and I'll be their Beloved and after I've charmed them, I'll allow them to woo Me, and I'll respond to their wooing as all beloveds respond to their lovers. And then in the beautiful last verse, lover and Beloved finally come together and the Divine Beloved hears the lover say, 'Darling, I love you', and they are One.

Beloved Baba knew we would forget Him, and He left His need in this song. He even allowed it to be played when He dropped his Form because it stresses the importance of how He needs us to know, He understands, and waits for someone to breathe His name and tell him 'I love you', as a true lover would tell his Beloved. He needs us to need Him. We should struggle to give Him His needs, just as He gave us our need by coming into the world. Loving is a two-way thing. If we go to Baba for His Darshan He gives generously and we in turn should be just as generous to Him, that is to struggle to love and to obey Him, repeating His dear name, bowing down His way, not our way. And offering all the thoughts that are in our head, and then repeating His name once we have given. No slander, no backbiting, no hurting others, in fact not only repeating the *Prayer of Repentance* but reading it very carefully and asking ourselves, 'have I done this'? And then struggling hard to not commit that sin again if we have. So, as we struggle, we begin to live the *Beguine.* We stir, and our hearts respond and the more we repeat His name the nearer we get to giving him His need ourselves. Baba is God. Let's all try to give Him His heart's desire and struggle to obey Him so that one day He'll come to us as a Beloved, and hear us whisper, for only Him to hear, 'Darling, I love you!'

The message in the *Beguine* renews the hopes and aspirations to further effort and struggle. We may not understand Baba's way of working but by effort and struggle and loving him more, we receive more of His grace and love. It is therefore an established fact, and Baba has left it on record, that he has retained the Presidency of the United Kingdom* having given up all other Presidencies. The United Kingdom holds a unique place in the world of today and the future, but if we are to see this in its true context, the greatest benefit any Baba devotee can derive from Baba's

Presidency is to allow Him to preside in our hearts.

*To clarify Fred's statement above: Baba, on settling some contrary opinions within the UK Baba group in 1956, declared Himself President of the UK Baba group for all time, or as He said: "in perpetuity".

***

Dudley Edwards, one of eight UK Baba lovers who attended the Great Darshan, remembers:

I was always struck by Fred's humility. Often when making a statement or paraphrasing Baba he would preface it with – "As I understand it…"

His flat reminded me of a monk's cell, as it was furnished with only the bare necessities.

I remember that, apart from Speaker's Corner, Fred would often frequent dangerous areas and mingle with unsavory characters to tell them about Baba. I can imagine that such was the strength of his connection to Baba that he was never in any danger.

Regarding the film - I do remember that there is a vague passage where Fred talks about following Baba's orders to acquire a record with Leslie Hutch's version of *Begin the Beguine*.

He told us about this in precise detail off camera. But when we tried to get him to repeat these words to record for 'voice over' he didn't seem willing to oblige, so frustratingly we had to leave the music in the film without explanation.

I remember a characteristic of Fred's was that when addressing anyone in his soft-spoken voice, he would often lower his head and peer up through his eyebrows as if he was looking over nonexistent spectacles. Fred was a very easy person to love and admire.

You will gather from the small amount that I can offer, that although Fred would open up to anyone about Baba, when it came to himself Fred was a very private person.

***

Karen Talbot, November 2023:

In the summer of 1977, during a week-long layover on my way to Meherabad and Meherazad I stayed at Oceanic, London, a house with many rooms owned by Peter Townshend. Followers of Meher Baba could stay there while in London.

One lovely afternoon, I met Fred Marks at a park in London. I remember that meeting because his presence was ethereal and filled with love and light. His loving essence has stayed with me throughout the years. Meeting Fred Marks was a highlight of my visit to London.

Meher Baba at the East-West Gathering, 1962

Chapter Ten - East -West Gathering, 1962

The heart that opens its door to a guest like Thee
The rest of Heaven's phoenix surely there will be.

The East-West Gathering was the culmination of three decades of work Baba had undertaken contacting His Western lovers, visiting their countries, and nurturing their inner links to Him. This unique gathering in India was an opportunity to bring them face to face with His Indian lovers under one roof, or as it was to be, one pandal.*[1] It was originally scheduled for seven days in November but was later reduced to four days owing to Baba's health.

MEHERAZAD
AHMEDNAGAR
22nd Oct. 1962

Dear *Fred Marks,*

My health is very bad but your love will help to support me during the days of East-West Gathering. Inform all in your party coming to Poona.

—MEHER BABA

Meher Publications
King's Road
Ahmednagar (Dn.)
Maharashtra State

ADI K. IRANI
Disciple & Secretary
AVATAR MEHER BABA

It was held at the Maharani of Baroda's Palace, Guru Prasad, in Poona, as it was then known. Charles Purdom recorded that one hundred and thirty-seven came from Europe, America, Australia, and New Zealand, another three thousand or so coming from India and Pakistan. Of all these there were few from the UK, but we know they included Delia DeLeon, Charles Purdom and Mary Parry, and of course Fred. It is well worth referring to the *Awakener*[*2] for a detailed account of the messages Baba gave out during those precious days.

Many noted that Baba looked much changed since '58, appearing heavier set and moving with some difficulty, but nevertheless it was estimated that He greeted upwards of 70,000 people, as many more came than were anticipated. It was generally not an occasion for personal meetings, though some like Purdom were afforded brief ones by Baba. Many of His long-time lovers realised it could possibly be their last opportunity to see their Beloved Baba and thus it was a very poignant time.

Fred recorded a series of memories which I will separate with asterisks, as they appeared on undated loose-leaf sheets:

Arriving at Bombay by boat, the P&O Liner *Currasia*, Baba sent word to me to proceed straight to

Poona. So, I took the train from Victoria Terminal, a crowded train packed with students and civil servants, and all kinds of workers. It was certain I was the only Englishman in the carriage. A young man asked me my destination. I gathered he had studied in England, and he insisted on ordering and paying for my meal. This visit was in answer to Baba's call for the East-West Gathering at Guruprasad. Jal had arranged for accommodation at the Napier Hotel – a dilapidated rambling building with gardens - which had been Poona Military Headquarters for Officers and N.C.O. staff. I liked the place.

Jal had me accommodated in a reserved compartment for the visit, being the first to arrive in India. Delia had arranged to stay with Arnavaz Dadachanji. Charles Purdom had flown by air and arrived later. The proximity of the Napier to Meher Dastur Road, as it was called then, was conveniently within easy distance of the environs of Baba's boyhood and youthhood. The nearby public gardens where he sat on the seats, the dusty streets with chickens flying and scurrying in every direction unheeded by cyclists moving in all directions. One is mindful of such humble settings as previously when Christ Jesus the Avatar was born in Nazareth in the

Holy Land, or as Buddha exiled from the Palace to the forest to be nourished by sweet herbs and austerity of fasting.

I gathered he ~~was~~ had studied in England. He insisted on ordering & paying for my meal. This visit was ~~the~~ in answer ~~to~~ to Baba's call for the East-West Gathering at Guru-prasad. Jal had arranged for accommodation at the Meher Hotel - a dilapidated rambling building with gardens. ~~and~~ which had been Poona military headquarters for Officers and NCO staff. I liked the place. Jal had me accommodated me in a reserved compartment for the visit ~~on~~ being the first to arrive in India. Delia had arranged to stay with Arnavaz. Charles Purdom had flown ~~travelled~~ by air and arrived later. The proximity of the Napier to Malet Castle Rd (as it was then) was conveniently within a ~~fortnight~~ easy distance of ~~Baba's Birthplace~~ the environs of Baba's boyhood and youthhood. The near-bye public gardens where ~~he~~ he sat on the seats.

The later years of the Ashram on the Hill and the Tomb seem bewildering but no less awesome. Similarly the days years later at Meherazad seem as aeons of timeless activity 'unmanifest', shining through the divinity of God on earth. What the lips of man cannot describe orally, nor the pen narrate for future posterity is still, and ever must be, confined and limited.

At Poona I did not sense the buzzing activity as felt at the Ashram on the Hill (*1954*). Poona was the place of Baba's birth - the birth of the One spanning the finite with the infinitude within his own body 'to the tips of his fingers', pulsating to the universal rhythmic beat, quickening humanity. Everywhere, yet somehow to a higher rhythm, like a fountain of pure sparkling water rising and falling to share and sustain stumbling humanity.

The capacity to believe is within every human form. A tiny spark might kindle the understanding of the true Mystic of any religion or of no religion. But who can bear within his frame the Infinite? Little wonder that He longed for one of us who would love Him as He should be loved. And that was a message He had sent out to His lovers everywhere.

*

There was a carriage way leading to the residence where Baba was receiving the East-West devotees from all over the world. On the left-hand side of the carriage way leading to the meeting hall there was a draped stall displaying books, buttons (*badges*) and information. I did not buy anything but glanced at the articles. Then a Baba button lying on the ground caught my eye. It was an old and much worn button. I put it in my pocket, forgetting all about it until arriving in the UK. I came across it in my travelling case. I examined it and noticed the photo of Baba was mounted on hard-as-steel metal, with a pin clasp soldered onto the metal disc, like a brooch, but at the top of the button a hole had been hammered through, disfiguring the top of Baba's forehead.

I've been asked many times for Baba buttons since the four days East-West Gathering at Guruprasad, Poona, but I never offered that button. I was always endeared to it. Baba looks as the Christ might have looked in the Garden of Gethsemane in Jerusalem. Baba, I fancy, similarly looks like the Prophet of Arabia glancing upwards, but which is disfigured by the hole hammered through the top, presumably to make it into a pendant. So, the owner had probably dropped it or thrown it away to buy another from that stall.

This button has always been my favourite one, but I could not pin it on my lapel, and yet I could never part with it. So, since that 4th of November 1962, it has always been close at hand. But several weeks ago, I glanced at it and the hammered hole is no longer to be seen not a trace of it. Why or how does not matter, but what does matter is that I can pin it on my coat lapel now.

Fred and Mary Parry striding towards Guru Prasad

We can supplement Fred's anecdotal experiences through those of other companions who also attended the Gathering. Whilst visiting Myrtle Beach in January 2022, I had the good fortune to visit Tom Riley who had just completed his autobiography, *More Light*[*3] He graciously allowed me to record him reading excerpts that related to times spent in Fred's company whilst there, and they are transcribed as follows:

My daily experience of walking and becoming familiar with Poona continued for almost two weeks before the commencement of the East West Gathering. Toward the end of October, Westerners began to arrive for this special occasion. Very soon the Pune Hotel was filled with Baba people. One of the first of these people was Fred Marks from England. Though considerably older than I, we became brotherly friends.

Continuing later from the same diary Tom recalls:

The first day of the gathering at Guruprasad beneath the pandal, Baba was seated before all of us, the Easterners, and the Westerners. The sky above was mostly blue with a few light clouds. Baba stood. A microphone was placed before Eruch. It was quiet. Baba's message was the following:

"In the event it rains, stay where you are, don't leave your seats".

People glanced at one another with expressions of confusion and surprise, because upon observing the sky above, it was bright and lovely. My chair was quite near Baba and I felt so blessed for this closeness to him. Sitting right next to me was Fred Marks from England. About a half hour into the occasion the sky began to transform. Large, dark clouds were ominously gathering, covering the blue and the brightness. Then began the sound of mild thunder, darkness increased, and rain suddenly began with intensity. Everything that Baba had said about not moving was instantly forgotten. In a moment many began to seek protection and find cover. They knocked over chairs, carelessly trampling over the earth, which was now turning to mud. Fred and I remained in our chairs amazed at what was taking place. Fred looked at me astounded and said, "Didn't they hear what He said?"

After the rain abated, Baba indicated that, in His love, He had purified the sanskaras of all present.

Through this experience of wondrous light and brightness, having been transformed into the natural chaos of dark thunderous clouds and rain, an alteration in sanskaric creation had occurred. Now a release toward purification and freedom had been initiated in all of us. What an unimaginable level of unbinding change! Thus, a new beginning would now be available.

As Baba said this I thought, how could that possibly be? Were this true, you would encounter an experience of freedom on unparalleled levels. How could that truly become a reality for us? The sanskaric impressions which have manifested what we are, and which have created an illusory reality, are suddenly altered into a pure beginning in which we experience a flawless now? I was perplexed.

Baba further stated that we were henceforth responsible for the actuation and control of all sanskaras in our lives. How to resolve within oneself such a challenge? How many are fully prepared to eliminate these impressions that bind? Through the practice of selflessness and purity? Baba wants us to take all the sanskaras that have limited consciousness and dwell upon their submission and their serious alteration, that is our mission. We then have the opportunity, since our old impressions have been cleansed, to arrive, to actuate the practice of limitation and control. Then our present and future impressions will have become wondrously recreated.

Continuing, Tom recalled another event:

On the third day, shortly after the conclusion of the morning session, everyone at Guruprasad left for lunch and I then had so much of the wonderful Villa experience all to myself. I knew of course that Baba had His quarters in Guruprasad, which was surprisingly large. I had the opportunity to explore the park-like landscape outside, which seemed to be all of two acres or more. I felt that I was alone here. I didn't encounter anyone in my exploration of the outside.

Within the Villa again now I was walking through a large high corridor with views to the gardens on one side and windows and French doorways on the other side. My experience was simply one of exploration. At one point my hallway was maybe fifty feet from meeting another broad hallway, when all at once three Western men appeared, turning the corner, and approaching me - Joseph Harb, Darwin Shaw, and Fred Marks. We greeted each other with happy smiles as they continued to walk. Darwin suddenly stopped and approached me. He said, "We have an appointment to be with Meher Baba now, come and join us, Tom."

I was taken aback, thinking who is he to invite me? Darwin immediately responded, "This may seem peculiar to you Tom, but as soon as I observed you walking toward us, I knew I had to approach you and ask you to come with us."

We walked back toward the direction from which I had come and passed three or four closed doors. One of the men then opened a door and we began to enter the room which was modest in size. A few simple chairs were in rows and facing an armchair. Meher Baba, accompanied by one of His Mandali, was seated in this armchair and smiling. Right away we sat down just before Him. He in no way seemed surprised at seeing us. Evidently this gathering occurred as a result of questions that had recently been discussed and required clarification now. I was only an observer.

The question put forward from one of these men was focussed upon one's need to actuate the longing to experience Baba's presence within oneself. Was it preferable or more beneficial to acquire this experience of longing by being in India? My recollection of Baba's response is the following:

"As my presence within you becomes more and more familiar to you there will be no need for you to return to India, none."

He communicated this emphatically as He moved his hands away from each other repeatedly, as though clearing away an obstructed pathway. I realised then that physical location is not necessary for the revelation of His sacred presence. His Reality must be discovered and realised within oneself.

How reassuring that must have been for them all knowing they would probably never see Baba again in His physical form after this Gathering, and certainly not again in the intimacy this brotherly group had allowed. It was indeed a most fortuitous and deeply significant meeting for Fred.

Returning to Fred's own recollections, the following two anecdotes reveal something of Fred's 'other worldliness' that left some of his companions bewildered:

When the East-West Gathering was over at

Guruprasad, Baba had left the armchair on the dais under the pandal, and suddenly there appeared a heavy cloud of rain. The Westerners jumped onto the dais and scrambled through past the curtain, and I was about to follow, but when I tried to get through it seemed as though limbs were flying about. Then Adi Snr sprang onto the dais, gained entrance, and closed the curtain. The huge crowd of Indian women devotees saw what happened. I suddenly was drenched with the heavy downpour and was standing on the dais with my thin cotton shirt clinging to my trunk. So having no other option than 'Hobson's Choice' as it is called in the UK, I began to cherish the soaking.

But as I stood, the crowd went panicky and were rushing towards the dais. Then among them, somewhere in the front was Ruth White aged 90, in a wheelchair. She was the only Westerner I noticed left there, so I tried to pacify the crowd by raising my arm in a gesture. There was a moment's lull and it all began again, and I was on the point of jumping off the front of the dais towards Ruth - she looked quite composed in a dignified manner - and then I heard someone call: "it's all right Fred, I'm here", and it was that dear Indian lady whom I had met in London, and whom Mani wrote informing me she would collect the favourite record of Baba's, *Begin the Beguine*, appeared to be quite cool. Her name is Naja Kotwal.

However, the cloudburst was over, and I thought about the coach that might by now have left. On walking towards the road, there it was, waiting to pull out with the party of Westerners being driven back to the Napier. Some were not pleased. As I stepped on the coach Ruth Stringer from the USA said: "Fred you'll get sent to the Tower!" I replied: "That is where the Crown Jewels are kept!" Then all was quiet, and the thought occurred, it is also the place where some were sent to be beheaded!'

*

Although I had arrived at Bombay several days before the meeting, Baba had sent word for me to proceed straight away to Poona, so I was first arriving in India and last to leave and I became aware of this when I was the last called to Baba and He said: "He's the first to arrive in India and the last to leave". However, I had to catch up with the Westerners returning by train from Poona to Bombay. The train was almost about to leave when heads appeared at the windows shouting, "Where is Fred?" I was looking up at a piece of the iron coping dangling loosely from the platform roof and which hung directly over one of the train carriage doors. While it was pointed out to the Stationmaster the party were all shouting and singing inside the train compartment, so I was indeed the last to leave Poona.

***

Janice Rieman, remembers Fred from the '70s when she spent time in London. (Janice worked for Bhau Kalchuri, Baba's nightwatchman, for many years in Kushroo Quarters in Ahmednagar where she still lives and now works with Bhau's son Mehernath Kalchuri):

Fred was a beautiful man with saintly qualities. I loved him very much and he was very important to me in our brief contact. He was really the one who first urged me to visit Adi. I met Fred at meetings at the Eccleston Square Centre, and I visited him once at his Putney Council flat. I love the beautiful image of him kneeling before Baba in that greeting-embrace line during the 1954 *Three Incredible Weeks* film.

Fred was actively attending Eccleston Square Baba Centre in Autumn of 1972 when I was in London for three months Sept - December. He lived in the Putney flat, after the Meher Manzil stay. I remember the people attending at that time were dear Delia, Tom and Dorothy Hopkinson, and Don Stevens (who was giving Monday night meetings), Sue Lane, Billy Nichols, and Barney, who was a friend of Pete Townshend and Billy. Dara and Amrit lived at Meher Manzil too after their marriage, and until after Merwan's birth.

Chapter Eleven - 'Pressing Forward'

Contented, like a tender bud in the heart's garden grows,
But in the crowd, it sheds its leaves, as droops the gathered rose.

When Fred returned from the East West Gathering he must have known it unlikely he would see his Beloved Baba again, but he knew his work was to continue loving Baba wholeheartedly and to share His messages far and wide. It is hard to fill in all the gaps in the absence of dated evidence, but I want to include these 'life fragments' that Fred sent to *Divya Vani* for publication in August 1965.[*1] They give a little flavour of Fred's life in Baba after meeting Him at six different gatherings in the '50s and '60s. These successive meetings exceeded most of his contemporary UK companions in Baba. They reveal how Fred was indeed 'pressing forward' as Baba had directed, and before many of us met him. The language of the text seems a little awkward, it may have been adjusted from the original for the Indian readership, but I have left it unedited as found at source.

Reminiscences of a Baba Lover by FRED MARKS

BABA SAYS: "Whatever I do is the expression of My unbounded Love"

In the early thirties of this century, Meher Baba first visited England. The event was then and ever since has been of incalculable significance, historical and spiritual. It was an historical event for London newspapers. At the request of some Baba lovers, He graciously granted two editors (one having since passed away) a series of interviews. To one who read the account[*2] as related in one newspaper at that time, the questions put to Baba seemed to be reaching intellectual summit level, significant of this age leaning towards spiritual truths, which can only be understood to some extent through the heart and mind! This interview was carried over to another day. In connection with these interviews, Baba had been kept for some time exposed in the bitter cold weather and was ill-clad for the occasion. That time Baba stated to His lovers that although He is God, being also human, He suffers as we do, if exposed to the cold weather. Twice Baba has reminded His lovers of that incident.

When the editor resumed the interview with Baba (it had previously been published), for further questioning he had engaged the most learned University Professor of 'Eastern Philosophy' available, to put further questions to Baba. Baba, no doubt has Himself created and sustained the whole of the proceedings for the sake of His work for humanity and posterity. Perhaps many readers came to realize that the Beloved is firstly and finally the trump and the ace of all hearts through the momentum of those interviews.

As we know Fred himself was the living proof that these newspaper interviews went straight to the heart of those who were spiritually prepared to receive them, as for Darwin Shaw and other early disciples.

The story of Richard Tanner

A Persian saying says: 'The man of God is a treasure in a ruin' - quoted from *The Wayfarers* by William Donkin. Until recently, living in one of the poorest districts of North London and for many years housed in a cold damp basement, a very poor man, in years nearly 70 was often seen in that district. He was loved by some and treated courteously by all in that locality. His name was Richard Tanner known as 'Dick'.

Apparently, he never slept on his bed which bore only a mattress. In later years, he would earn his living in some simple way, sometimes helping to sell newspapers in the severest of English weather. With

the newspaper he would include a small, printed
pamphlet with a message of Jesus Christ. A Baba-
lover, *[Ed. i.e. Fred]*, lived in the same district,*[*3]* and
occasionally Richard would call upon him. Here,
Richard first saw a photograph of Baba. In the same
room he reverently revealed that Christ appeared to
him in a vision. Richard also glanced at a cupboard
and remarked: "The regalia is in there"*[*4]*. Actually,
what was kept in the cupboard were papers and books
relating to Baba.

Richard began spreading Baba's message and
telling the local people quietly who Baba is, although
he had not yet met Baba in the flesh! He had an urge
to obtain slides to stimulate people's interest through
showing them with the aid of someone at a Mission
Hall, and for that purpose he would often point to an
old lantern projection in his room. Because of severe
privation and prolonged suffering, his health gradually
failed. Later he received assistance from the
Government and moved to a nearby hostel. His friend,
[Fred], had for some years moved to another part of
London, but one day while on a visit to Richard, he
was seen almost on the point of collapsing in the
street. He was taken to a hospital and in later years to
two other hospitals. Towards the close of his life a
badge with Baba's photograph was given to him. It

was evident that he was refreshed and cheered to have such a treasure. He was very indignant, when a sister at the hospital removed it from the wall at his bedside where he had affixed it to the light switch.

He wrote saying, 'I had a vision of dear Baba. He spoke to me, so He will be greater than all the doctors as I know He will cure me of my illness. That is a fine thing to know. Dick.'

Shortly, after he once again returned to the hostel, a phone message was received on Saturday 22nd May 1965 saying that he passed away on the previous day, Friday 21st May 1965.

Hospital Patients hear of Baba

Invitations have been offered to Queen Alexandra Hospital, Putney, London through the Secretary of the Friends of the Hospital Association. The patients are wheeled in a chair to the large hall and an informal talk is given *[by Fred]* as to who Baba is and His Universal Message. The questions asked are to the point and intelligent.

When Adele Wolkin was passing through London on her return from India (where she had been nursing) to the USA, she attended one of these meetings. She told the patients that her uncle was a specialist in USA, on arthritis. A patient who had heard of Baba only once before, immediately asked Adele: 'Have you told your uncle about Baba'? During the short talk, the rest of the patients in the wards could hear through earphones connected with the amplifying system.

London Newspaper Interviews

Recently, two Baba lovers, *[Fred, and Hoshang Patel]*, interviewed the editors of several national newspapers in London. Visits were collective or individual as the circumstances arose. For a whole week, and for several hours daily, the editors took interest, and some became a little alarmed at hearing of Baba and whom He claimed to be, and of His solution for God's worn and weary world. That there is a solution for humanity's problems is readily and sincerely agreed upon, by responsible people constantly in touch with the mundane affairs of the world and the interviewees were left with that impression.

The western religious attitude, in varying degrees anticipates some kind of advent of the Christ or Godman to manifest anew to the world. However, it cannot agree as to how Christ WILL manifest. The newspaper editors being more practical and intellectually inclined, (and some of whom say they have previously heard of Meher Baba), stated that they meet and freely discuss 'such matters'. Their problem is, as to how they can put it into print and convey it to the masses of humanity. During an interview, one editor was told that his graver responsibility lay not in the fact of his publishing that which some people not only believe but also know, that Baba is the Christ, but on the contrary failure to do so would be his personal responsibility. That Baba is the Christ, as undoubtedly He is, was not challenged and neither was His message. However, having left one interview to proceed to another, the lines of Tennyson seemed to ring in the air of Fleet Street -

'Theirs is not to reason why!' (*The Charge of the Light Brigade*.)

Taking a Stand

On foot in Putney High Street, London, with a silent prayer to Baba, I proceeded to a spot suitable for such an occasion on Saturday, 29th May - rayed in sunshine and equipped with a loose paper cover of one of Baba's books and a copy of Baba's Universal Message both neatly displayed inside a transparent plastic holder, and a bundle of Baba's Universal Message folders, counting 39. So began the stand at 2.00 pm, three yards away from the stream of by-passers and congested road traffic. To each, who by chance took a glance, his eyes fell on the only gesture: an outstretched hand holding a single folder, the other hand pointing to Baba's dynamic message to humanity on the loose paper book cover.

The first enquirer, a young woman, remarked: 'I seem to have seen his photograph before somewhere'. So often heard, this remark intrigues. The answer it seems is that Baba is both the Beloved and the lover. An outstanding instance of what is mentioned happened when, one carrying Baba's photograph on the lapel of his coat and waiting in a bus queue, was challenged with the sudden question from a young woman: "Is that a photograph of God?" The answer was swift and sure: "Yes, Christ on earth—Meher Baba!" The first enquirer was offering to pay by dipping her hand into her purse while asking for the folder but was told: "This Message is from the heart—nothing to pay—I thank you for accepting it!"

Then a fair-haired youngster, about 7 years old

came over and smilingly asked for a folder. His mother looked very pleased as she waited for him. Being a child, he appeared unusually interested. Another recipient was a fair-haired youth in his late teens. His face lit up with a smile, he held three half-crowns asking the price. The reply was "Meher Baba's Message is of the heart, so there is no money to pay!"

On Saturday, June 5th, with the same equipment and a handful of folders counting 27, I took the stand again, the onward and outward gesture being as previously. On this instant an African woman asked and quickly walked away with the Message. Now an Eastern visitor looking over, said to his friend audibly: "Meher Baba!" He hesitated but received the Message and hurried away to catch his friend.

A middle-aged woman, who came and asked for a folder was informed: "This has the Message of Meher Baba!" She was seen going in the stream of humanity and the last glimpse showed her with the open folder and kissing the photograph of Baba.

Here is a dialogue. An elderly lady approached and stood near to me. "Have you lived in Barnes?" she asked.

"Yes", I answered. "Baba's brother lives there. Mr. Adi S. Irani". She received a folder saying, "I will take this to my friend. I am flying over to see her. She lives at Staten Island, New York. She always puts me on top of the world. She is 83 years old but does not look more than 60 years. Whenever I see her—I feel on top of the world." I enquired, "Who is your friend?" She replied, "She has volunteered full time at the World's Fair, New York. Her name is Mrs. Zarahdo Bahjejian. She went to India".

"They call her Auntie", I said. "The folder you received is (*same as*) from the Baba Booth at New York World's Fair."

"That is where my friend is. Oh! I will keep this myself." she said. The lady's name was Mrs. Carlisle. Mrs. Zarahdo Bahjejian was at the Napier Hotel, Poona during the Sahavas in November 1962. She shared an apartment there with Marion Florsheim. How devoted they are to Beloved Baba! I was at the Napier at the same time.

All but one of the folders had now been passed on and this was asked for by a poor aged lady often seen in the district. Quietly she said, "Isn't it time for the Lord's Coming?"

The publication of the foregoing anecdotes in Divya Vani were enabled in India by Adi K Irani but Adi also managed Fred's personal correspondence to Baba over the years. A series of letters held in the Trust Archives provides touching insights into the intimacy that Fred shared with Baba about his homelife and particularly the care of Baba chappals which he mentions on more than one occasion.

On 16 March 1966 Fred writes:

'Baba's sandals which were brought to England by Will Backett are in my care. They are on view at the monthly Group Meetings held here in London.

My present job during the past fifteen months is making tea during breaks for a team of men on constructional work in Central London.

Filis has notified me of receipt of manuscripts and is pleased with them. Yours in Baba's Love, Fred.'

It then becomes apparent Fred is moving house 'there not being sufficient facilities for attending to a large amount of correspondence', and on notifying Baba he receives a reply from Adi saying:

> "I read your letter to Beloved Baba and He says He is with His dear Fred and wants you to keep happy in His Love. He sends His Love and Blessing to you."

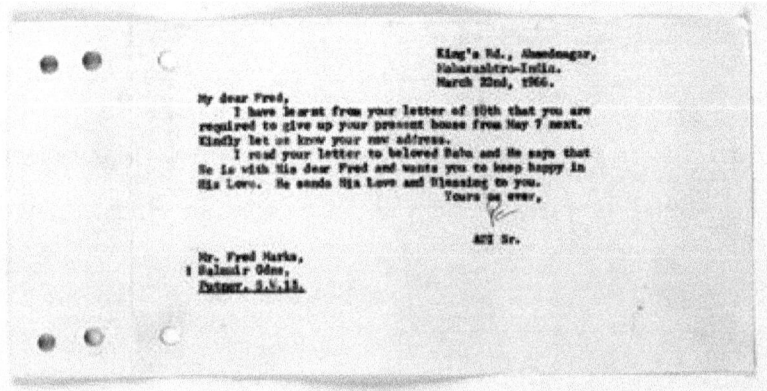

There then follows a three-page letter from Fred to Adi, dated 4 April 1966 outlining in some detail a project he is proposing - to distribute Baba's Universal Message and Books to the public, and he details the costs of printing 750 notices regarding the monthly meetings he is scheduling to achieve this. He then describes his new accommodation including the detail that the key to his rooms must be left with his landlady when he is away, but states:

> Until Baba tells me to relinquish the sandals, I am sure I should have the key to the room where they are kept.

I take them to the monthly Group Meetings where they are displayed in a small box.

[Handwritten note: Until Baba tells me to relinquish the sandals I am sure I should have the key to the room where they are kept. I take them to the monthly group meetings, where they are displayed in a small box.]

Fred then details at length the background of the other tenants, his landlord, the rent, and the removals and continues describing the accommodation:

It is a semi-basement with outhouse and toilet, and an entrance from the back garden. For several days I have been doing repairs and renovations. Expenses have cost about £80 but I hope to recover some from the landlord. I have bought a small desk and there is a built-in cupboard for keeping Baba's sandals. The right of entrance is solely the tenants and I feel I can comfortably attend to correspondence here and elsewhere.

[Handwritten note: It is a semi-basement with out-house and toilet, and also entrance from the back garden. For several days I have been doing repairs and renovations Expenses have cost about £80 but I hope to recover some from the land-lord I have bought a small desk and there is a built-in cupboard for keeping Baba's sandals etc. The right of entrance is solely the tenants and I feel I can comfortably attend to correspondence here and elsewhere.]

Fred, perhaps still concerned that this might not be suitable or secure enough for Baba's chappals continues:

May I add just one thing. If Beloved Baba who

evidently cares so much for me decides otherwise that I look elsewhere for a room, I shall be very happy to do so.

Dear Adi, will you convey all my love to Baba regarding His care for me.

Through this handful of letters, we witness how Fred deferred to Baba on every aspect of his life. No detail was overlooked. And he did indeed fulfil the project he had described. We will never know how many souls he introduced to Baba on the streets of London. One letter to Mary Parry in Bradford speaks of ordering hundreds of copies of Baba's Universal Message to replenish supplies - Fred and Will giving these out on street corners and in public buildings in London, and Mary Parry distributing them in her home city of Bradford - despite being shunned by her family for her conviction. What great courage they had spreading Baba's message in these ways!

***

David Lee, a long time American Baba lover living in London remembers Fred:

I knew Fred and feel very blessed to have had the opportunity, however briefly, and to hear his stories about Baba and spend some time with him at the Centre. He was kind, gently spoken and powerfully focused on his devotion and love for Meher Baba.

I was teaching at a school in the East End of London, and we were on an outing to the Museum of London in the city. I was one of the supervisors of our diverse group of young people. During our midday journey to the museum, we travelled on the top deck of a double decker bus, passing through the very busy streets of the city. As I was looking out the window I saw Fred, standing quietly on a corner with a placard around his neck that had sayings about Baba. He was a brave and great channel for spreading Baba's name.

On another occasion I made a visit to Fred's home in Putney. I travelled with Ann Collette, and I think Lol. I can't recall who else was in our little group of four, but we travelled in my car from north London. We sat for some time with Fred in his small room. He was such a gracious host. We had a very special meeting together and he also showed us various items in his possession from his time with Baba. It was a wonderful visit I shall always remember. On returning to our home the car was flooded with light from our visit. There was a remarkable atmosphere filled with a deep abiding presence of Baba. Everyone felt this and we had such a strong sense that we had been in the presence of a deeply spiritual individual and that Baba had been present and was following us on our journey home.

Chapter Twelve - Fred's later life

There is much cause for trusting when in despair -
the night is absorbed into the morning air.

By the late '60s in the UK a stalwart group of longtime Baba lovers had established itself in Baba's service. They included Delia DeLeon, Adi and Franey Irani, Molly and Douglas Eve, Tom and Dorothy Hopkinson, Olive Pitt, Don Stevens, Maud Kennedy, Ken and Alice Lawton, Mary Parry and of course Fred. They held regular meetings in various venues in London, usually organised by Delia or Fred. The numbers attending were few. Suddenly a group of young Baba lovers, mostly artists and musicians, burst on the scene in the late sixties at the very moment the hippy movement was at its zenith. Baba's message of love resonated in their hearts, and they were swept up in new and creative expressions of His Divine energy. Many of them met Fred during their early years in Baba and some have contributed to this book.

This new generation of Baba lovers had barely begun expressing that love through their music, art, and publishing projects when they received the devastating news that Baba had dropped His body. All grieved the fact they hadn't yet seen Him physically as many had been planning to attend the scheduled '69 Darshan. (Eight of these young lovers were inspired nevertheless to attend the Great Darshan in May.)

(l-r) Dallas Amos, Barbara Amos, Sue lane, Dudley Edwards, Georgina San Roque, Craig San Roque, Christine Cook, Martin Cook.

Among this new Baba group was Pete Townshend who was to establish a dedicated Centre for Baba on the River Thames, (Oceanic), where many gathered, including those in transit from the US to India. The Centre opening was blessed by a gift from Baba's Mehera of a pink silk coat which is now housed in the London Centre at Hammersmith Grove.

During this new phase of Baba's manifestation flourishing in the UK, Fred continued to hold regular meetings and was recorded by Irwin Luck who was visiting London from the US in 1971[*1]. Though his talk references events that have been included in previous Chapters, there are new comments and insights arising through the passage of time.

Fred speaking:

Darshan

Before I met Baba in person, I believed He was God on earth before I went to India because of the work, inner work, that He had accomplished. He gave me the experience of feeling that He was undoubtedly the Saviour. When I look upon Baba, I feel that He is my personal Saviour, not so much a guru or teacher but a Saviour. I believe the world needs to be saved and I believe it can only be saved not by teaching, but One like Baba who has the power to save.

When first I went to Him, I went with an open heart because Baba invited me to go. I felt that in knowing everything I could go with all my weaknesses, knowing that I was understood, and when I met Him face to face I felt 'here is God on earth'. I forgot all about the West, and Baba took very little notice of me among the others. There were 17 of us present that period from the West, but I felt that all the time I was like a sieve and that He knew everything about each one of us, and about me, all at one and the same time. Once he called me to Him privately. He didn't ask me a question. He said: "You know who I am, I am the

Ancient One, once again I am drawing my fishermen to me. You are very dear to me."

On another occasion He said: "Press forward, do not think that you are being neglected."

To be more accurate He said: "I do not want you to think that you are being neglected."

My experiences of Baba are so varied, sometimes loving sometimes the reverse when I've been away from Him. The most vivid experience I had in Baba's presence was one day at Ahmednagar in the ashram. All the others that were present went out on a charabanc, sight-seeing, but somehow, I remained behind and Baba came along, and I felt in the presence of Baba they were the most sublime moments of my experience in Baba's presence on earth. There were no questions to be asked and we were alone, and I've always felt since that in quietness Baba is to be felt. Very little is learned through words.

Another time I was in physical contact with Baba at the Darshan in Ahmednagar when those thousands of people came to Him, and for some reason I was drawn to Him, and I was sitting next to

Him, and I was given a cushion to shield His back every time He leaned forward to give each one prasad. I put this cushion to His back, He only had His sadhra, nothing else as it was very hot. Baba was perspiring and this was to keep His back shielded from any draught. So, during those hours I saw much of the service that Baba gave as He served humanity, leaning forward and giving prasad. The following day I could hardly move my arm, and so I wondered how Baba could go through that ordeal of serving people and giving prasad, having garlands placed upon Him, thousands of them, and the work that He was doing.

As said, when I went to Baba, I went to Him believing that He was, and Is, God on Earth, therefore there were no questions; but Baba did once, I think, cause me to ask a question. I sat there with the others and was prompted to ask Him, "Baba, is love limited to the form or does it go beyond the form?"

And Baba threw up His arms and he said: "Infinite, infinite!"

And that conveyed much to me, and I felt that Baba prompted me to ask that question for some reason to get beneath the surface of my consciousness.

To be relieved of the burdens of life and the problems whatever they be - mentally, physically or spiritually - I believe that we can unburden ourselves in this lifetime. Baba has now dropped His body, and His work (although as I understand it, He has returned to His exalted place), His work continues intensively and I believe this is the time for us to unburden ourselves with the possessions, attachments or whatever we feel, if in any way depressed or oppressed.

The young people from America draw my attention to a photograph *[Ed. taken during the '54 Darshan and used on the cover of this book],* so I will explain the happening that led to the photograph. It shows Baba with palms of His hands to my cheeks. It happened this way. It was during the day when Baba was giving Darshan to an endless queue of people, but there was a moment when a woman, a very poor woman, put the least coin of value known as a paise at His feet. Now Baba pushed this away into the sand and rubbed it into the sand with His foot. Baba stood erect and it seemed to me there was something passing through this Divine Being, some kind of agony and it so touched me that for some reason I was drawn nearer to him and although the Westerners were near too and watching, I went to Baba and He touched me on the chin. I ought to have gone on my knees because being tall and Baba was now sitting at this moment, I was still a head above His form, (that is what I regret in the photograph), but Baba said in that moment:

"This needs no discourse."

So, it conveys a meaning to me. I don't know why I was drawn to Baba but since that time I often visualise Baba suffering in that position as He looked at that moment, and I feel myself standing as He stood. And often it comes to my mind what Baba was going through, and I think it draws me nearer to Him, and to love Him more and more.

Working with Adi, and Obedience:

The time came when I had a letter from Baba. It was in connection with Him asking if I would be obedient to Him, and some months afterwards another, regarding the work that I was to do for Him. I was to work with Adi Junior in London to help him in His business. This was an act of obedience to Baba. A letter was sent to me, and I read it to Adi, and the experience of co-operation almost, in partnership with Adi, often brought me in conflict with my own ego in obeying Baba.

Adi Sheriar Jnr., Baba's younger brother and Fred's business partner.

```
                                        Meherazad
                                   24th October '66
Fred Marks (237 Upper Richmond Road, Putney, London SW 15, U.K.):-
BABA  WISHES  YOU  HELP  ADI  EVERY  POSSIBLE  WAY  TO  YOUR
BEST  CAPACITY  IN  BUSINESS  PROJECT   LETTER  FOLLOWS
BABA  SENDS  LOVE  AND  BLESSING  TO  YOU   STOP   SHOW  THIS
TO  ADI  FRANEE
                          = MANI =


Dear Fred,
              Above is copy of cable sent to you this morning as
instructed by Beloved Baba.  Baba further wants you to bear in
mind dear Fred that you should under no circumstances let Adi
down by giving up half-way in whatever business project that
Adi starts with your help and support, but continue helping Adi
throughout the project to the utmost of your ability.
Baba has instructed Adi to try his utmost for some opening for
further earning, taking Baba's Name, and He wishes you to help
him in every way possible.
              Beloved Baba sends His Love to you His ever dear
faithful Fred.

              With love in Baba, from all your Meherazad family,
```

We are accustomed to loving Baba in our own way, and that is good and proper up to a point; but often it can be the way of the ego, and mercifully Baba brings us away from a tangent and puts us on another proper and rightful course where we learn the

lessons that He alone knows that each one must learn -
the lessons that He alone knows.

Adi and I both have love for Baba: we express it
in diverse ways. The time came for me to forget Baba
and put all my energy into working with Adi. I was
learning from Adi and Adi was learning from me, and
Baba was to be the coordinator of all the energies that
we put into our efforts, so that the experiences that
come through Baba sometimes try us to a point of
desperation. Some of the experiences are full of joy,
bliss, and happiness. Sometimes one can reach a point
of calamity when one's faith is tested. Whatever
calamity befalls, a Baba lover must not lose faith in
himself; Baba is his true self.

Some curious anecdotes

Each time that I've been to India or America
Baba has sent instructions that I must go by boat. I
didn't understand the purpose of this but afterwards I
saw it was for the work that I had to do on the boat.
For instance, on one occasion I sat in the lounge on
one of the P&O Liners and I saw passengers
discussing a committee they were forming, a sports
committee. The captain of the crew was there - his

name was Captain Christian - and a woman was talking, and she pointed to me and said:

"He will do," and she came over, pointed to me and said: "You will be the chairman of our committee."

I learned it was the sports committee and it was something I knew nothing about, and I'm not interested in, and I told her I have no interest in it. But she pointed to me again and insisted, so I became chairman of the committee.

During the sports sessions that occupied several weeks, I had to stipulate certain things, make rules about gambling and so forth. These were against my principles, and also apparently against the ship's rules, and so they were ruled out by my vote. I saw the purpose of this: I'm reluctant to join in any organised work.

Once, when we were in India, we were on a visit to Sakori and some of the disciples were held up by a breakdown. There were three of us present I remember - Baba, Charles Purdom and myself, and we stayed and waited for the others at a tea stall on the way. Baba said:

"They won't be here for some time yet; they won't arrive till evening, someone tell me a story."

And I could never think of a story. When I'm with Baba I can't speak somehow, I feel that Baba has taken the power of speech away or I have no use for it. So, Charles Purdom told Baba some jokes.

Adi interjected at this point in Fred's talk and related the story of a joke he had shared with Baba. There is apparently an old Indian saying that the taller a man is, the more he lacks wisdom. In 1954, Fred, William and Mary and Charles Purdom were together and Fred stood out, being tall and striking. Adi repeated the saying to Baba in Gujerati and then asked Baba 'does this saying apply to Fred?' Baba laughed and reportedly said: "No, it doesn't. He comes to me with love in his heart, so no matter how tall he is, he doesn't need this sort of wisdom, he has love wisdom."

So, another wonderful affirmation of Baba's love for Fred reported by His own brother! Moving on...

In 1976 Pete Townshend was inspired to commission a film[*1] about Fred, which was made by Martin Cook and Dudley

Edwards, two of the '69 Great Darshan group. The narrative on the film focusses on reincarnation and I include the transcript of Fred's words as spoken.

Fred:

It was always at the back of my mind that I wanted to seek and to search. Where am I going from here? Death is something which is part of life. It is a continuation of life only in another form. We should not grieve over a person who has passed out of this life because it is selfish of us to want to attach ourselves to the body of a person as it were. Actually, it is selfishness, we are grieving about the body, we want them to be with us you see, and yet that is not what we really love. What we really love, or should love is the soul, and the peace that they enjoy. We should not fear death, this transition between life and death is just another state of life, of consciousness. The person passes out into another phase, and he leaves the body behind, the body of suffering, and he enjoys for a time, a life of bliss.

There is a period when he again has to come into the life of illusion and take another body in incarnation, and we should look upon this life as a life not that is real, but a life of illusion. Baba says, 'God alone is real', so until the whole of the person's impressions of his previous life are worked out, or wiped out, by the grace of the Master, he has to come and take another incarnation. It would not do for us to know the past because of the things done and left undone, and God mercifully cuts our consciousness between knowing our past incarnations, but He knows them. Meher Baba knows a person's incarnations right from the beginning of time. One can incarnate into parents that are suitable for the incarnation of the soul for it to carry out the impressions that it has to go through and carry out. What I would say to every person, as I understand the teachings of Meher Baba, every human being gets the best possible parents under the law.

It helps to pray for a person who has entered into the transitional state from this life into the next, but after the first three days it is not effective. The soul leaves the body after either the first or the second or the third day, but rarely after the third is the soul attached to the body. So that God never leaves us, He is always present, ever present.

My eyes dropped on this tombstone, the first one that I saw. The words on it are very appropriate.

It says:

'In loving memory of Tom Richardson, Surrey, and England cricketer. He bowled his best but was himself bowled by the best.'

Something we all have to meet sometime, to get bowled out. Baba was a very good cricketer, well, all-rounder. I wasn't acquainted, neither did I like the game at all, and they made me the captain. This was when I was at the school, or just left school and I was about 17. And the only good thing I did in cricket; there was a swift ball going over my head and I put my hand up and I caught it, and they said it was the best catch they'd ever seen, and it was a fluke too!

If we could become childlike in our nature, in every detail, every moment, we would have that ability and that childlike innocence. A bird in a cage has never known what freedom is. A human being cannot understand the spiritual freedom that Baba gives. His soul is encaged within his physical body. Freedom is not understood, in the sense that there are many kinds of freedom. There's political freedom, religious freedom, national freedom, and racial freedom, and many other kinds of freedom which are all limited in their scope. But the greatest freedom of all is the freedom of the soul which includes all the other freedoms. The reason people do not seek consciously the freedom of the soul is because they are not aware of it, or that it exists. And that impels them to seek freedom in other directions. If I want a better world, I must become a better man, then the world for me becomes better.

Man dreams about material perfection and the more he thinks about material perfection, the less he thinks about God, until he thinks God does not exist at all. Baba is the pivot of the universe, and the universe depends upon that which comes forth from the Godman. Baba is the God almighty on earth in our lifetime. Every movement of his finger, of his hands meant something. I happened to be there once with him alone and I had no need to ask questions or anything. It was sufficient to be in that quietness, knowing who He is. The love of a devotee is a gift from Baba to the devotee. Humility or humbleness is also a gift from the Master. It is not something that one can use at any time and bring into play. It is a virtue, a spiritual virtue, which saints possess. Baba has explained to us, he has given us an instance of dust, and how it can be trampled on, how it responds to any treatment that is given to it. And He says we have to be like dust, that is to be humble.

Where The Godman walks, every atom of the earth there is blessed. When one loves a Master, all things become new to him. Even his environment can change, which hitherto had been best for the ego to express itself in, through the work that the devotee was doing, or through a man's profession or whatever it may be. Baba helps everyone to overcome the ego so that they find a more congenial attitude towards life and towards their fellow men.

Baba wanted the *Beguine the Beguine*[*2] record by Leslie Hutchinson, so I thought, well Baba wants this record then surely, I must find it. The words were

240

already there, and Baba only needs the instrument, and Cole Porter was the one.

Baba's methods cannot be understood because no amount of intellectual explanation can explain them. They are infinite, and they are always for the good of humanity, and always for the good of the individual. Meher Baba says everyone is destined sooner or later *(for the goal)*, so we should have patience, try to overcome our fate in this lifetime, and look towards the goal.

But let us remember that it is all illusion, it is only love that is real and that God is love.

We believe Fred returned to Meherabad twice in his later life accompanied by friends from his Thursday group, Lol Benbow and Michael Lakey. From correspondence in his keeping, we know he was warmly welcomed by the Mandali.

In 1978 Fred returned to Myrtle Beach and was a guest speaker there. We know from Anne Barker's recollections that Fred made an impression upon her, and doubtless others too. Here is a brief excerpt from the talk he gave:

I thank you all for coming along to listen to me.

As Baba aspirants and lovers, we are destined not only to work towards bringing about our own individual emancipation through Baba's grace, at the same time we are, in so doing, also sharing with Baba His work in bringing about the 'New Humanity'. Baba has stated he intends to direct the tremendous energy of the US into constructive and creative channels. Therefore, the USA has a unique place among the humanity of the future. The magnitude of Baba's work is beyond imagination, but the devotee's emancipation has a bearing regarding His work because the devotee is in the vanguard of the new age. The generating energy released by a nation of so many cultures in an age of highly developed technical achievements inevitably leaves a gap between the heart and the mind of the individual. In a mixed-race community, there are many fine spiritual qualities dormant within the individual, and these among other factors Baba intends to awaken in the individual.

Baba states faith is something we have, or we do not have. The question is whether it is a weak faith or a strong faith. In the world of illusion all human activity is generated in part by desire and a blind faith; that may apply to humanity in general. But there are untold instances of man being an agent of the Divine will, unaware that he is an instrument for some Divine purpose whereby the course of history is decided upon.

The constitution of the USA was formulated by a few men on the principles of justice and the rights of its people. In the illusory world however, all values are in a perpetual state of change amid the flow of time, and in this sea of apparent chaos, the Baba aspirant has to take a firm stand and be steadfast in his work for Baba, always having in mind the essentials of love and obedience. If we feel obedience to be some specific personal order from Baba to his devotee, or even if we are not aware of any specific order as such, we should still hold on to Him and not let go of Him. That, in a way, is being obedient, and there are endless ways of loving Him and in loving, one is being obedient. Baba says, 'Don't worry, be happy'. In some measure that is an order to be obeyed, but Baba, least of all, is undemanding and He knows the weakness and the strength of each one of us.

In notes for other talks Fred gave late in his life in London he continued in a similar vein. His emphasis had shifted from the personal growth of the spiritual aspirant and his own inner journey, which we see in evidence in the following *Experiences* manuscript, to perceiving Baba's lovers as workers for God. As such his talks became focussed on urging those he contacted to experience themselves as active in unfolding Baba's New Humanity as this small extract reveals:

> As Baba aspirants and lovers, we are destined, in whatever part of the world we happen to be, to share in the God-given task which Baba set before each one of us. The greatest and most powerful force and example that any Baba lover can devote to Baba is the stand he maintains through Baba's grace and guidance. Throughout the world there is a cleavage to the old order due to desperation and fear. Baba's plan, divinely ordained and eternally maintained for the New Humanity, Baba has entrusted to those of us who are in the vanguard of the progression of an enlightened, new way of life, which no longer seeks to maintain the old but yield to the inflow of the new.

> To help others through one's own example, one must get not only thoroughly drenched, but drowned, in love. As a prelude one should attempt to create a balance between thoughts of the mind and the feelings of the heart mind, however mind works much faster. Baba's love is with his lovers always, helping and guiding them. Work undertaken with honest intent and love for God is Baba's work, and those who do this

are always His. Hafiz the poet declares, 'A thousand times I have ascertained and found it to be true that the Universe and the affairs of the Universe are totally nothing into nothing. There are two things, truth and law, truth belongs to God, law belongs to illusion. Give up all forms of parrotry and start practising whatever you truly feel to be true, and justly to be just.

If Fred's intention through his talks was to inspire others to take up this challenge, then a measure of his success is more than adequately reflected in the hearts and minds of those who have offered their memories for this biography.

***

Martin Cook, the photographer and filmmaker, remembers Fred:

Fred lived for some time in a shed in Adi Junior's Garden in Barnes before gaining a council flat in Putney. Meher Baba directed him to work with Adi in the Antiques trade, Fred does refer to Baba placing opposites together in his notes. Fred was very placid and Adi very fiery.

Fred was at some time in the Coldstream Guards.

One time Fred acquired some money, £50 pounds, I don't know from where, but he told us that he didn't know what to do with it and he placed it in a red Royal Mail post box. I have no more details as to whether it was addressed.

During our audio recording of him in Richmond Park, Dudley and I were asking questions to build ideas for the film that Peter Townshend had requested. During the reel changeover Fred informally said to Dudley, 'trees have souls', and said that he could see them. On renewing the recording tape, he was asked to repeat it, but he said that it was not for the tape.

Fred was very humble and shy but did his duty, he used to go to 'Speaker's Corner' at Hyde Park and give out Baba's messages to passers-by.

Fred knew the woman who was my first Baba contact, Mary Parry. They travelled together to the *American Sahavas* in 1958 in Myrtle Beach. We found out that the Centre thought they were married and had put them in lodgings together. Mary told us later that they didn't let people know, but Mary in her 'uncertain time' would often say to me that she would marry Fred!

Part Two

Experiences

I have deemed it my good portion -
to have been born poor of this world's fortune.
Yet, in this fate of 'ups and downs'
I played the ace of Baba's clowns,
And found no mirth in the Kingdom of Earth.
But now I know that I am Thine,
God's Kingdom's come,
and Thou art mine.

Fred Marks

It Has Pleased the Master to Inspire Certain Passages In this Book.

Fred's Foreword:

In this book, it is not my intention to try and expound the Teachings of Meher Baba. It would be like holding a candle to the sun.

Meher Baba is not what might be generally understood, as that of being a man of God, neither is He a man from God. He is God Himself in human form.

It is felt therefore, that in writing I cannot by any standards do justice to the Master. To love and serve Meher Baba as He should be served, is equal to serving God and the Universe.

When the whole of one's being is entirely taken up in the service of God, there would remain nothing more to be said. It is not for the purpose of introducing anyone to Him, strange though it may seem, for He has stated He needs introduction to none. (This should be understood in the spiritual meaning.) He Is the Ancient One from whom we have come away, and to whom all consciously or unconsciously long to return.

For those who have already come in line with His teachings, they may find little interest in this book. It is offered to anyone in authority, to the outcast and downtrodden, the rich and the poor, to those who feel hopeless, and to all who feel oppressed or depressed in any way whatsoever, and to the 'sinner' so-called, for whom, Meher Baba states, He has principally come – of whom the writer feels he is, and in the sight of God, that and no more.

Fred Marks, Autumn, 1977

Introduction

In a letter dated 15th September 1978, Fred wrote to Dana Field stating:

> I have been busy putting *Experiences* into book form. This is now complete. It was not until important Baba Mandali told me to write that I so decided, so now I have to think of an Editor and Publisher.

It is clear from a subsequent letter to Filis Frederik that she requested the manuscript be sent to her, as on 19th January 1979, Fred writes:

> I was very happy to receive your note. The delay in answering is due to a belated perusal of the manuscript which Pete Townshend and Mathew Price asked for.

Soon after, a letter to Filis reveals the manuscript had indeed been sent to her as, on 19th June 1979, Fred wrote:

> I hope you are well. Also, I write to remind you of the manuscript you asked to be sent to you, and later in my letter to you, asking for confirmation that the manuscript had been delivered to you. I have received no reply.

Doubtless in the busyness of her life it was a project for a later date, and so it was that Fred's manuscript remained dormant in Filis' Archives until 2021. Almost half a century has passed. Whilst today this collected biography will probably be read by those who already know of Meher Baba, it was written by Fred primarily for those who do not. At times it may seem naïve, and the language of its time, but if we read it appreciating the challenge posed to Fred by Baba's Mandali, we can only feel deep appreciation for the love he expresses through his *Experiences.*

Index to Experiences

In Search of God

The human being seeks happiness, first in the home, he seeks God in the home, though unconsciously. The height of happiness is to be found in the love of God. So, he says,

'Where is God, is He in the home?'

So, he leaves home and parents to search unconsciously for God.

Then he reflects upon those whom he left behind in the home, who were also seeking happiness, which at its height is the love of God. So, the world is a world of God's children who are born into the world seeking reunion. For a few it becomes in real earnest.

In Search of God

The human being seeks happiness, first in the home, so he seeks God in the home, though unconsciously. The height of happiness is to be found in the love of God. So, he says, 'Where is God, is He in the home?'. So, he leaves home and parents to search for God. Then he reflects upon those whom he left behind in the home, who were also seeking happiness, which at its height is the love of God. So the world is a world of God's children who are born into the world in search of God. With a few it becomes in real earnest.

The true Lover is one who has found what he sought. The

would-be Lover is one who is ardently seeking what the true Lover has found. Between the two there is a difference not in love but in ability. The one who has ability seeks arduously, never thinking for one moment I must consult before I do, but doing. This is true love. The one who seeks, says 'This can't be wrong, but I'll see what someone else feels first'- this is not true love. It is love being guided by another, who probably knows even less than the seeker, and therefore the seeker is given wrong advice.

Always tell God what you need and then go ahead, and He will tell you 'Do' or 'Don't'. If you need Him. tell Him 'I need you'. If you want Him, tell Him 'I want you.' Give Him a little more so that He can enter your mind and tell you much more.

Baba States in *Discourses - Maya, Part One, False Values*: People pursue their happiness through everything except God, who is the only Unfailing Source of Abiding Joy[*1].

'Who Am I?'

If the question arises at the back of the human mind, 'Who am I?' or 'Whence and Whither?', it invariably remains in a state of abeyance and unresolved. If, however he searches deeper and still deeper, he may be imperceptibly led to find an authoritative answer. But for the world over, it invariably takes shock or a real crisis in a human life to bring about a momentous turning point. It is most natural therefore for one to search deeper and to bring the intelligence to focus on the question.

It is easy to abandon hope and drift aimlessly and waste one's precious lifespan; especially when laws are framed to simplify, yet falsely make life easier for one's pleasure and self-satisfaction, even at the cost of moral, physical, and spiritual consequences.

When this happens on a grand scale a reverse is sought by way of dealing with such issues as separate departments of human life, moral, mental, and physical. For instance, take an infant child denied the love of its mother to which the child has a divine right; it begins a life with an irreparable handicap. The spiritual aspect of man must arrest and equip him in his entirety to enable him to be made whole.

Our besetting deeply rooted ignorance can only yield to the touch that kindles the spark of spiritual understanding, that there is but One God the Beloved, and that humanity and all life has sprung into being as the object and expression of His love. Love needs expression and reception. It is justified of itself and is beyond all other considerations. All life is

256

sustained and maintained by it.

> 'Who Am I?'
>
> If the question arises at the back of the human mind 'Who Am I?' or 'Whence and whither?' it invariably remains in a state of obeyance and unresolved. If however, he searches deeper, and still deeper he may be imperceptibly led to find an authorative answer. But for the world over, it invariably takes shock or a real crisis in a human life to bring about a momentous turning point. It is most natural therefore for one to search deep and to bring the intelligence to focus on the question.
>
> It is easy to abandon hope and drift aimlessly and waste

In True Love words are so precious, they are most eloquent in silence. But, if they come up and escape the throat, let the words echo the language of the heart:

Baba I love you. I love you Baba!

True Love hears. When there is no sign or lead, then give love for the sake of Love.

Who is Meher Baba?

Meher Baba is Avatar, the descent of the Deity into Incarnation. He is the Ancient One. What are his attributes? He is All in All to all men. What is he? He is that which each one takes Him to be. To some He is Saviour, to another He is Teacher and so on. Is He the Christ? He is the expected One and can be none other than the Christ, whom the Christians are waiting for. How shall they know He is the Christ? They will know when He manifests.

Who is Meher Baba?

Meher Baba is avatar, the descent of the Deity into Incarnation. He is the Ancient One.
What are his attributes? He is All in All to to all men.
What is he? He is what each one takes him to be.
To some he is Saviour, to another he is Teacher and so on.
Is he the Christ? He is the expected One and can be none other than the Christ, whom the Christians are waiting for.
How shall they know he is the Christ?
They will know when he manifests.

The Divine Incarnation

The Avatar is the unseen God of man before He comes down to earth to be One with all men and to be worshipped by men. Baba's object in Re-incarnating was to bring to the World Himself, Who adores.

Now this Man we know as Meher Baba is called Avatar, which of course means God, and Avatar has a duty to those who adore God, and that duty is to show His lovers how to love, not by giving gifts, but by sacrificing comfort.

The Avatar's comfort was NIL throughout His life on earth. He suffered for the World as did all previous Avatars, and it is for the Love of God that the Avatar suffers. We must therefore try to see Him not as a man, but as God sacrificing comfort for God.

The All Knowing

In this unique period of the twentieth century*, *[*Ed. as written]* the Avatar has disciples, aspirants and devotees both Eastern and Western, of whom many had been drawn to the Master through the religion of their birth. The five great religions comprise Zoroastrians, Hindus, Buddhists, Christians and Muslims. Each religion is named after its founder who was Divinity, or God in human form at that time. Each one appropriately became known as the Prophet, Messiah, Saviour or Messenger, or whatever was a suitable presentation for the deliverance of the Humanity at the time.

For our period, the twentieth century, Meher Baba has not come to teach but to Awaken. He is therefore known to many as the Awakener. But He is no less Saviour and Prophet come again to redeem Humanity. He is All in All to each one and all. He imparts, according to the spiritual aspirations of the individual, that which is best suited to his understanding. A glance from the Master, or a benevolent touch has the power to transform one's life. He 'speaks' in a new spiritual potency. It may be timely advice, or it may remain somewhere in the recipient's consciousness and come to the level of awareness at a time when it is most necessary, even years later, at some time throughout one's life.

It may, therefore, be inferred that Meher Baba is the Oversoul, or the Soul of all souls and the knowledge He imparts is unerring.

The Spiritual Hierarchy

The whole range of the spiritual hierarchy has been clearly set forth and described in the book *God Speaks*[*2] dictated by Meher Baba to chosen editors. This book describes step by step, in the minutest detail, much of which formally has been lost from sight, or in part known. The recording is entire and absolute and is brought to a state of perfection for future reference and for posterity.

It describes, by bringing into intelligent terms of understanding, the almost abstract primordial origins of matter during its earliest stages, formerly possessing the condition of fluidity as a gaseous substance.

It is drawn along in an evolutionary course, simultaneously evolving in form and consciousness in an effort or urge to know itself and become conscious of its original source. It proceeds changing from one form to a higher form during its finite illusory stages of evolution, retaining at every level its previous latent consciousness, until it has advanced throughout the stone,

260

vegetable, reptile, bird, animal arriving at the human form, which Meher Baba states is the final.

In its final emergence as the human being, man is still not aware of his true self as real and indestructible. The final realisation takes place during the ensuing metamorphosis from the human stage to the divine. But in the human form, consciousness of man asserts and eventually affirms or denies the existence of 'God'. The Godman asserts His independence as the First without a second and, for the advent on earth, takes the image of man during His incarnation. No less so is man made in the image of God. Meher Baba has come to awaken us to our true source and relationship with Himself.

Meher Baba, the innermost and outermost in each one and all

The general attitude towards what Humanity calls 'God' is that of having blind faith. It may be a strong or a weak faith. It may be firm and constant and invariably determined by one's creed. Belief in God may continue through obscurity and undampened by adversity, and for humanity in general it becomes apparent that man goes through life consciously or unconsciously in some degree of spiritual apprehension, awaiting his acceptance of divine revelation. He awaits a measure of proof. When the Avatar comes, that is the proof for Humanity. The Avatar is synonymous to the whole of

Creation, for each one and all. Man should therefore not only believe, but long, strive and yearn for the new life. If he finds it, he has found what life is all about. If he does not succeed, what will he lose by it? By preparation he will have found himself in a state of readiness.

But in the minds of many people today arises the question, 'who is Meher Baba?' Many have seen His photo, read some book about Him, or some seem to have heard His name mentioned.

Others say, 'it rings a bell'. The truth is that He is not an ordinary person unless it is to be argued that Buddha, Krishna, Christ, or Mohammed were ordinary men, each, in their own day and cycle.

Meher Baba is the superhuman Divine force which touches the hearts and souls of Humanity today, over the globe. Every cycle has its Avatar, and Meher Baba is the Avatar or Messiah of this age, the Ancient One come again to redeem humanity.

Baba bestows grace without becoming less Himself. His message that we should love Him in everyone and serve Him in each other, is alike in meaning and significance to the saying of Christ:

In as much as ye have done it unto one of the least of these, My brethren, ye do it unto Me.[*3]

The Teacher

The greatest teacher is he who teaches in silence through the living example, who by the living word, rather than the written precept, dispels the darkness of our minds, who sows the seed of love in our hearts to be tended for the time of harvesting, and who prepares the pupil forthwith to shine in the common ways of life.

It is He who becomes the living message and torchbearer for mankind with heart and mind vibrant and harmonious in action. The purpose of this book will be gathered in from the summing up of the reader himself.

The life of a man is lived, and accordingly the good and the bad are consequently both revealed or concealed in obscurity. However much he may voluntarily or involuntarily manifest his life outwardly, it is bound to move along its course prescribed by the two opposites of good or bad.

Meher Baba, the central theme of this writing, is not however
concerned with man's life as aforementioned. He goes far, far beyond it.

The writer knows through experience that the sting in the life of the past is removed by the grace of Meher Baba.

The mind's impressions (sanskaras)[*4] of the past become fainter and fainter to disappear for ever, not by passing into a state of forgetfulness or the storehouse of memory, but by life's slate being wiped clean for ever by the Master's grace.

From having let go the hold on the past, there springs an implicit joy-filled adoration undiminished even by a sense of unworthiness, however, at having received such forgiveness and blessings. So, the reader is presented with life as it is, life as it could or should be, and primarily how it may become so.

Equality and Importance

There are the rulers and the ruled in the world, and from the prevalent materiality, power and authority amongst humanity come various upheavals. Yet, amidst it all there is that which recognizes the need for some sort of authority to provide stability through LAWS, for the further well-being of the people. In this respect it can be seen that all authority is not equal.

At the same time human beings, as soul, are all equal. Less known to the world at large, however, are the spiritual forces which prevail throughout the universe, and which have a direct and indirect bearing upon all life forms on earth.

It is to be understood that all life and indeed the universe itself, is entirely dependent upon the sole authority which stems from the Avatar when He is on earth; or from the Qutub-e-lrshid[*5] when the Avatar is not on earth and who, with the other Perfect Masters, is responsible for sustaining the LAW - God's way.

It is the spiritual hierarchy, which in its unerring functioning, is constantly gearing life on earth on to a higher level or quality of life. Its authority is unchallengeable, and it is also instrumental whereby no man, woman, or child, nor any form of life, is completely isolated from its benignity.

When the Avatar is to make Himself known, He descends to the Seventh Plane and is stationed there until He becomes aware of Himself. Then He 'tells' God – 'I must move my station' - if He needs to perform miracles. If He does not need to perform miracles, He usually establishes Himself on the Seventh Plane. The Avatar never descends to the gross plane of consciousness for if He did, being Perfect Man, He would become perfectly gross and therefore not able to work Divinely for humanity. When He descends it is to function as a Perfect Man, and that function is more easily performed on the Seventh Plane.

Jesus was stationed on the Seventh Plane but when He performed miracles, He stationed himself on the Fourth.

The God-man incarnates because the five Perfect Masters who are on earth at that time draw Him down. They tell Him, 'Sir, the time has come! We are ready for your incarnation as Avatar', and He comes.

The Avatar needs no man's help in His work, but He allows man to help because it gives those who help a spiritual push. These people who help are mostly unknown to the world, and are developing the consciousness of the subtle and mental planes and are known to Him as the Hierarchy. These are not necessarily people in His immediate circle and, except for the five Perfect Masters, have no authority, but they carry out the will of the Avatar, or Qutub-e-Irshid if the Avatar is not on earth.

When the Avatar drops His form, He is no longer required to function as God on earth. He therefore hands His key to the Qutub-e-lrshid, and from the moment the Avatar drops His body, the universe becomes the responsibility of the Qutubs. They are 'God in Form', equal in authority to the Avatar and capable of carrying on the work for the universe.

Pressing Forward

Having come to Baba it becomes certain that He does not want to know, nor does He interest Himself in a person's past, whether it be success, failure, or achievement. Nothing, if He so choose, I believe, can pass His surveillance, past present future of anyone or anything. For instance, it is my belief that He knows the moment of one's birth and the moment of one's death. But how would it help? Would it enhance our faith? All along He satisfies, but not our curiosity.

With conversion it seems the shades of pre-spiritual life become lighter and lighter until there remain no shadows. Baba has made this point clearly understood when He states, 'When you stand direct under the sun there is no shadow.' It seems certain that what He does see is the extent to which the devotee loves Him. Love for the sake of love awaits neither sign nor signal.

love for the sake of love awaits neither sign nor signal.

The Significance of the Heart

The endless knowledge to be had regarding mind and body might appease the average intellect, but where mind and heart are involved, a more balanced and fruitful search for the deeper aspirations become necessarily involved, and these are akin to the well-being of the soul.

Man is unable to create divine love for himself. It is bestowed by God. Neither is man able to create the human love which transposes human affairs and transactions. All love flows from God, and for the sake of Love we are told He created the universe. The vaunting posturing of the human being is endless in the search for truth and happiness. In the light of Meher Baba's teachings there is lucidity enough for us to understand intelligently that we, including the whole universe, are absolutely dependent upon God.

Meher Baba explains:

Divine love makes us true to ourselves and to others. Divine love is the solution to our difficulties and problems. It frees us from every kind of binding. It makes us speak truly, think truly, and act truly. It makes us feel one with the whole universe. Divine love purifies our hearts and glorifies our being. Divine love is qualitatively different from human love. Human love leads to complications and tangles. Even the highest human love is subject to the limitations of individual nature.

Divine love is matchless in majesty. It has no parallel in power and there is no darkness it cannot dispel. It is the undying flame which has set life aglow[*6].

Taking God Seriously and Life Lightly

Baba said: People take life seriously and God lightly, whereas we must take God seriously and life lightly."[*7]

What does Baba mean? Let us consider the implication of sex relationships between male and female. It is the most misunderstood of human relationships, and because it is the most subtle it allows, and gives scope for, manoeuvring of human behaviour. In the human being it reaches full development, but its scope is unending. Because God is not taken seriously, it follows that human relationships on all levels are never secure and remain eternally something to be striven after, and even when achieved offer a temporary feeling of happiness and fulfilment. There is never any way of making anything absolutely and finally tenable between human beings.

Trust and faith, goodness and kindness and goodwill, and many other virtues play a great part in making life bearable. These however are qualities attendant upon circumstances arising throughout all human relationships and transactions during life on earth. That which has a beginning must also have an end. Even human love has its limitations. There is always the question of faith which cements human relationships in every field of life throughout the world. Yet the quality of faith and trust is subject to endless unknown factors. So, the tenure of human life on earth is never certain.

When you begin to love God, you do not fall in love. To take God in a light manner and go through life as though He does not exist, even though one may believe in God in one way or another, is like putting the seal of authenticity to one's own fate, good or bad, which determines the course of one's life on earth, in the final hope of some happier existence after death. Baba's teaching assures humanity of life's purpose which is to love God and to be useful to one's fellow man. Baba says He has come to open wide the gates of heaven. This is God's gift to humanity and to take God seriously and

270

life lightly is the beginning of True Love.

> Baba's teaching assures Humanity of life's purpose which is to love God and to be useful to one's fellow-man. Baba says He has come to open wide the gates of heaven. This is God's gift to Humanity and to take God seriously and life lightly is the beginning of True Love.

Trust and Faith

Everyone has trust. In the tiny baby, the baby is unaware of its trust. The baby has trust, but it is in the form of instinct and consciousness as feelings towards its parent. This in turn endears the parent to the child. The parent loves the child through its responsibility to it and is instrumental as God's agent for bringing the child into the world. Parents become the guardian and protector of their child. In turn, the child turns towards its guardian, and both become attached and possessive towards each other. The child grows and flowers into youth. All are God's children but by far the most give up the search for God. Does man trust? Yes, and in countless ways. There is nothing in the whole world which does not trust one way or another. Trust hinges on expectation.

Baba informs us that the stone ultimately informs the human form. The dormancy in the stone is so torpid and it is so undeveloped it neither asserts nor claims, but trust is there in complete abeyance as its sleeping partner. For one to entrust means to commit or confide to a person's care; consequently, that person becomes charged with a responsibility, duty, or care to its charge. Can the Baba lover aspire to love Baba as St. Francis loved Jesus?

Among the divine qualities that go to the heart of Baba, St. Francis possessed these two, love and humbleness, and a third which is always stressed by Baba, that of obedience. What is unique regarding Baba? Divine uniqueness is in Baba's expression: 'I am the Divine Beloved who loves you more than you can ever love yourself.' It is expressed and communicated at the same time to the one who can receive it.

I AM THE DIVINE BELOVED WHO LOVES YOU MORE THAN YOU CAN EVER LOVE YOURSELF'

To give thanks may be an expression in words, but if it were to thank God as he should be thanked, every moment of our lives would be such an expression. To feel grateful and thankful for something received should go to the heart of the recipient, and the giver shares in having been able to give. True love is an expression of the heart. Every time you and I breathe in the air, that also is a gift from God, but it is taken for granted, and we are not conscious of our breathing until we become short of breath. Why is there so much uncertainty and chaos in the world as of today? Because one aspect of man's relationships towards his fellow human beings is that of trust. In all his affairs, the true welfare of man depends upon mutual understanding, the reciprocal of give and take. It is so simply dependant on faith and trust, but it is a blind faith and can never be considered as absolute, and therein lies the uncertainty.

Man's trust is determined and assured by confident reliance on firm expectation, which depends upon the one of those who has been accepted, and in whom reliance has been entrusted. To be able to rely in confidence gives a measure of repose because of the trust placed in the trustee who is considered deserving of that trust and confidence and is not liable to fail in time of need. In this age of materiality, where man dreams the dream of making material the object of perfection, the trend in human nature is reflected in the world of mundane affairs when man's principles and standards continually play hide and seek to evade law and order, which brings about disruption throughout the social structure. The decline gathers momentum, and fear of painful apprehension of worldwide upheaval creates a state of alarm which spreads over the world. Humanity becomes affected and fearful and instrumental in bringing about the very thing it fears.

Selfishness, which in the beginning is the father of evil tendencies, becomes, through good deeds, the hero if its own defeat. And when evil tendencies are completely replaced by good tendencies, selfishness is transformed into selflessness, that is individual selfishness loses itself into universal interest.[*8]

The Law of Karma

'As ye sow, that shall ye also reap'[*9]

Here on earth men exercise authority. A king rules with authority over his subjects. Now, according to Baba, it may so happen that a king may be a bad ruler or a tyrant. In his next incarnation he is paying the dues and demands of what Baba describes as the inexorable law of karma to which everyone is subject. In its working it exacts the living out of an opposite experience to compensate the swing of the pendulum, in compliance with the law of opposites through which the law of karma operates, and which determines the course of life, and which can overrule the plans of man. And so, Baba explains, 'the bad king who misruled or misused his power, must become a beggar in his next incarnation, and it so happened that one of his trusted servants who served him in his previous incarnation now held forth his hand to offer him a coin'. What a tragedy! Both king and servant unaware of their previous connexion.

And so, Baba in the published Discourses states:

'Everything and everyone in the universe is constrained to move along a path which is prescribed by its past. There is an inexorable 'must' that reigns over all things, large or small. The principle of 'must' which overrides human plans is based on Divine Law. It is only Divine Will that can supersede the Divine Law.' Divine Love is above all laws and Baba has stated: 'one who lives for himself is truly dead, and one who dies for God is truly alive.'[*10]

Freedom from Binding

The visible established order, so called, has no permanent basis, wherever it happens to exist in the world, but it is not remote from the various avenues by which men search for some measure of freedom and happiness. Baba in His message to the youth of today states the encouraging fact that there is always something in the world to merit their love. A youth may leave home because he does not find sympathy there with his highest aspirations. A youth may find that in his search for what he considers his highest ideal, there may be frustration, even pains of yearning and longing to discover the object of his adoration. But if home and parents are entrusted by God as human vehicles to enable souls to incarnate, behind it all there is the search for happiness even by the parents.

Each and all are searching for freedom and happiness in his or her own way, but it is only transient, and when collectively pursued, each contributes in their own way that which unwittingly, or knowingly, builds a pretentious and established edifice. Limited however are the freedoms pursued, whether they are political, religious, national, or racial. Baba's call is to the life of the spirit, where all men are extremely important and for which, Baba states, all are eventually destined to arrive finally at the goal. Only spiritual freedom carries the stamp of divine authority, for it is the freedom of all freedoms. The others are always subject to the ever-changing circumstances and prevailing influences in the world. Beyond the ever-changing visible forms, and beyond the bounds of human intellectual capacity of itself alone to understand, Baba has come to make us aware of the invisible and indivisible and eternal oneness of which He has stated, all are one. Baba declares:

"You and I are not We but One!"*11

Spiritual Conviction

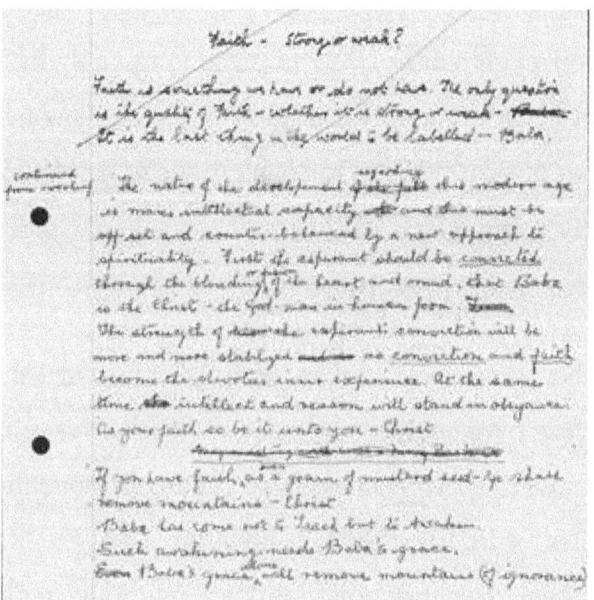

Fred's early thoughts on Spiritual Conviction.

To become a Christian, one turns from the bad to the good and from good to God to find that God is love. It is not sufficient to believe in Christ. One must be convicted. In conviction, the heart goes to the mind, or the mind goes to the heart. However, one influences the other. The unyielding tenacity of the respective followers of each religion where rituals and ceremonies become formalised, only yields to the touch of Divine Love and the kindling of the spark of true spirituality for which purpose all religions came into being. Meher Baba has not come to found yet another religion, neither has He come to teach, but He has come to Awaken.

Prayers offered to God can be a part of religion or independently offered to Him. Regarding prayer Meher Baba states:

What matters is your heart, the prayer that arises from your heart, that is the prayer that Baba hears, that God hears.

In the inner spiritual panorama of the universe nothing is more sublime that a spontaneous prayer. It gushes out of the human heart, filled with appreciative joy.

The ideal prayer to the Lord is nothing more than spontaneous praise of His being. You praise him, not in the spirit of bargain but in the spirit of self-forgetfulness. *12

278

Baba Keeps Silence

From the 10th July, 1925, Baba informed His disciples of His intention to maintain Silence, which continued over the years. It was sustained throughout, during arduous working on all levels. His silent messages were translated by Eruch Jessawala, one of Baba's closest Mandali, who followed with unerring skill Baba's fingers gliding swiftly and gently over His alphabet board, which was held in His left hand. The message or statement of whatever import was proceeding, or for anything immediate at any moment, was readily conveyed.

Baba Keeps Silence.

From the tenth of July 1925, Baba informed His disciples of his intention to maintain Silence, which continued over the years. It was sustained throughout the years simultaneously during arduous working on all levels. His silent messages were translated by Eruch Jessawala, one of Baba's closest mandali, who followed with unerring skill Baba's fingers, gliding swiftly and gently over his alphabet board, which was held in his left hand. The message or statement of whatever import was expedited and imparted for whatever work was proceeding or for anything immediate at any particular moment.

But whether Baba was giving timely advice, granting a special interview or imparting discourses to groups, the human mind is unable to grasp the time factors. During the autumn of 1954 He gave up the use of the alphabet board, continuing giving messages by hand gestures and a flexibility of facial expressions which conveyed to the beholder some transfluent divine treasure which when received by the interpreter the substance became intelligible to go straight to the heart and mind.

But whether Baba was giving timely advice, granting a special interview, or imparting discourses to groups, the human mind is unable to grasp the time factors involved. During the autumn of 1954 He gave up the use of the alphabet board, continuing giving messages by hand gestures and a flexibility of facial expressions which conveyed to the beholder some transfluent divine treasure, which when received by the interpreter, the substance became intelligible and went straight to the heart and mind.

Forgiving

In the common way of the life of the world, the friction, ill-feeling, the hurts given and received and the pains arising out of maladjustments between people, have to be deeply felt and understood in their spiritual meaning: that what one does to another, one does to oneself. If it is understood that God's nature is mercy, and if man is to be blessed, it behoves him in the common ways of life to show mercy and forgiveness to his fellow human beings.

On one occasion Meher Baba sent for the writer to go to India to attend a special meeting. I went with an open heart. For almost a month, other men from the West were also present. The immediate change from the intensity of the West to being in Baba's presence caused me to forget my life's ups and downs. I was completely absorbed in attention toward the

Master, from whom however, nothing could be hidden. I considered myself to be the least deserving of all those present. Yet I was aware the Master was screening my faults from the other participants. Such is Meher Baba's compassion. This proved to be the master 'key' to rid myself of my weaknesses when I returned to the UK.

> Teach me to feel another's woe,
> To hide the fault I see,
> That mercy I to others show -
> The Mercy shown to me.[*13]

Nature

Nature, with a capital 'N' is God's servant; that is within the realm of nature. But man has a separate nature, and it is his own nature which he must overcome. Every individual nature finds expression through instinct and so the saying arises that a man is constituted by his nature. In human beings no two natures run parallel. The nature of a person is the instinct through which his life is expressed for his own gratification and his attitude towards life in general.

It is not Nature as God's servant which man must overcome. It is his own nature or his natural instincts. Nature in man seems to say, 'I am in your keeping, I am your servant as instinct, the outcome of which serves him right or he gets his just deserts'. Whilst always at his bidding, instinct thus makes man a slave.

When the life of the spirit takes hold of the man, his instinctive nature causes him to dilly-dally, to loiter or waste his substance and time. Baba has given us the example of the metamorphosis of the chrysalis emerging from its encasement. Nature gradually recedes for the release of a higher form of expression as light and warmth draws beauty out of its prison-house into buoyancy and utility. It is a stage of higher manifestation. Baba has come to awaken, so that the spirit of man may shine forth once again in its pristine glory!

Fleeting Happiness

The fleeting happiness of human life, or the sudden and unexpected reverses, become accepted as conditions for human existence which is life on earth the world over. It is to take things or life as it comes. It would be futile to 'kick against it.' The open gateway however leading out from this earthbound existence of unredeemed spiritual life is to have a belief in what one considers to be for the highest good. It draws upon the imagination of man but is far, far beyond it. Yet it is to be seen or felt, or to some extent imagined in the life and example of the Godman.

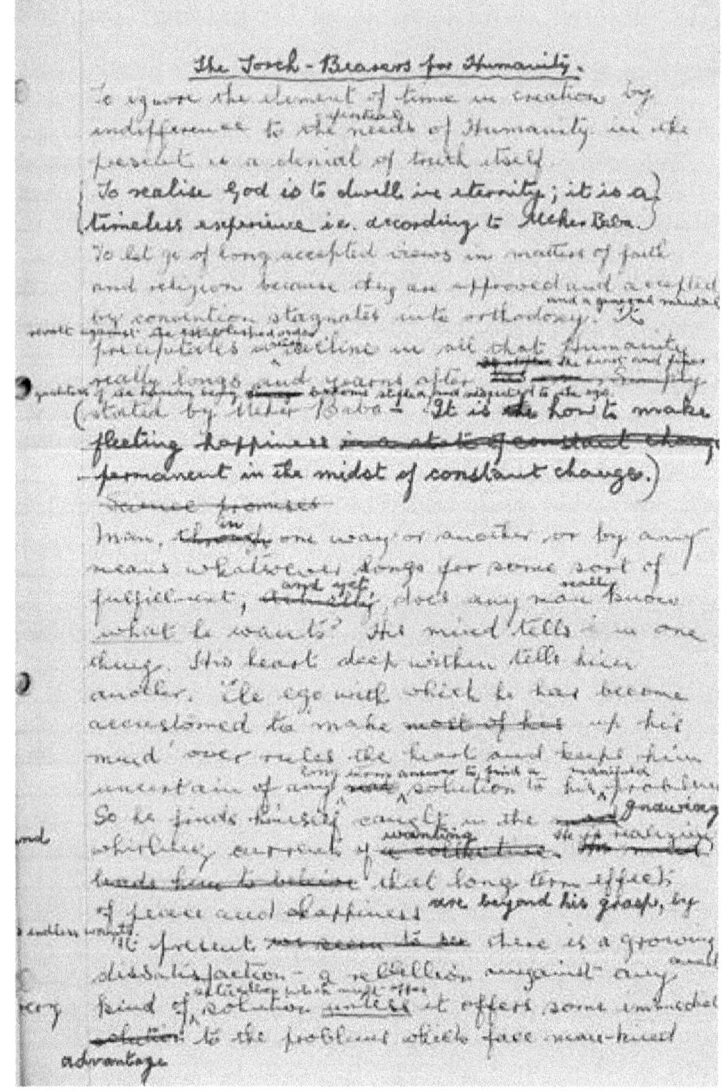

Fred's early thoughts on Fleeting Happiness.

Christ as infinite goodness became for man an example of the highest good. The real spiritual significance of Christianity has yet to be realized. There was no time when humanity was without the divine example. It is certain that in our lifetime, the twentieth century, *[Ed. i.e. when written]* Meher Baba has come to remind and help us to become aware of the impending manifestation of God, having first demonstrated the divine example expressed through word and action during His lifetime on earth.

Morals and Law

When life is cleansed of unending sense impressions of self-gratification, it opens up a new range of action for serving the Master, or Humanity. Serving the Master is no less serving one and all. Life is geared up to a new level, which becomes the rallying point for which the quintessence of the ancient and ever renewing spiritual principles can operate and motivate the devotee's life.

The truth of all religions is there, but the theme of religion alone is unable to recapture the imagination that will enable man to aspire above the materiality which prevails in our day and age. To touch the mind and heart, an individual needs the grace of the Master, who loves the aspirant more than he can ever love himself. Such an occurrence happened in the life of the Apostles of Christ or in the divine romance affecting the life of Mary Magdalene whom Jesus high-blessed with Divine Love and rescued from a life of degradation and despair. If an individual is to become free from the enslavement of immorality, it is essential that he becomes wholly and entirely new, spiritually. The morals of a person are therefore a side issue. A person does not become a better person through laws, either by passing new laws or by reframing old laws. A person becomes a better person through Love.

From Belief to Conviction

Belief and Conviction

When the muscles of the heart become strong, through its new found Love in Baba, there is a stronger urge for the pilgrim to aspire from belief to conviction. When the pilgrim is convicted of the divine status of Baba, his mind can no longer sustain its doubts over the heart respecting the validity of Baba's divinity. The former conflict between heart and mind is resolved in spontaneous Love served by the mind for discrimination in the daily life of the pilgrim.

The marriage is between heart and mind and not necessarily the distance between the physical presence of Baba and the pilgrim. Where there is Love, Baba states, there is no separation.

Hold on to My damaan - (garment.)

Baba

A man was the owner of three dogs. One followed close at heel. The second alongside its master. The third kept well ahead of its owner - first running, suddenly stopping, and turning to keep its eyes on its owner - then off again.

Fred's early thinking which transformed over time into the following statement.

The man who categorically believes in the existence of God, may remain bound in consciousness in both mind and heart; functioning, even though his belief may embrace some outward form of religion.

In this restricted state of mind and heart, the events and experience of life are bound by what Baba describes as 'the inexorable law of karma.' The individual consequently functions under that law. Also, the mind, imposing itself upon the heart which also has its own functioning in the life of the spirit, has acquired and become accustomed, and to some extent submissive and subservient to, the dictates of the mind, functioning and circumscribed by the karmic law.

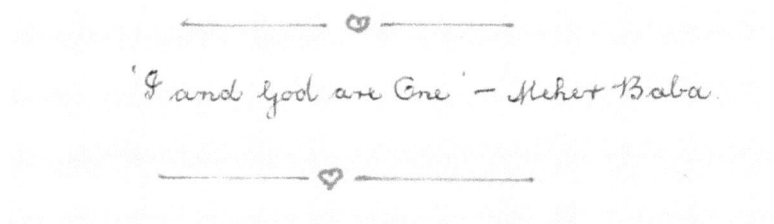

'I and God are One' — Meher Baba.

But in conviction of God, that consciousness becomes unbound, and the heart awakens, through which the man begins to experience the true Self and receives glimpses of Truth. It ensures man's revival and removes the idea that Beloved God is far off and unrelated to man and his affairs. Meher Baba has come so close that humanity is being stirred from belief into the conviction that God not only exists, but also that 'God Is'.

Paramount in importance for the spiritual life of man, if he is to have lasting peace and happiness, is that he must be awakened and experience beyond proof this awakening brought about by Meher Baba.

Following conviction therefore, the unity of the heart and mind functions separately but harmoniously, and here man stands unassailable by doubts, possessing proof beyond argument.

'I and God are One' – Meher Baba

Knowing

Knowing is love. Divine love knows all. Divine love IS. Why? To know God, one must love. To know how love IS, one must know Self. Self and I are One. To know God divinely one must be One, and to be One, one must adore. How? Adoring is loving to such degree that one is not even aware of loving. It is an act of supreme obedience arising from 'I'. This means 'I', the supreme 'I' or higher Self which knows itself. It is 'I', and I am God is knowledge of the Self or 'I' – 'I' IS', is the essence of being. 'I am' is knowledge.

Knowing 'I' comes after a long period of knowing how to obey; obeying Baba so implicitly that one would never think of disobeying. 'I am' is knowledge of God as one's true identity. 'I IS' naturally follows 'I am'. 'IS' is being. 'Am' is knowledge, and the two go together hand in hand.

God IS. 'I' IS. Not 'God and I' but 'I and God are One'. 'God and I are One' means God. The all-powerful and all-knowing God, and I, the form is One. That is the knowledge of One who has reached the goal 'I AM'.

I and God are One means that 'I', the higher self, and God are One in being - that is the knowledge of a Perfect Master. 'I' and God are One. God IS, therefore 'I' IS.

Point of Contact

How can you and I experience something which we seemingly never previously found or experienced, and yet restlessly feel as an imperative need? At long last how is this mystery to be solved not only by words but in experience?

You and I have inherited within the soul, that which also stirs the soul. That 'something' dormant, asleep within the heart or soul, must be awakened into expression in life. Baba's ways are infinite through which He is bringing it about - as many ways as there are human beings.

288

If you love me with the love St Francis had for Jesus, you will not only realize me, you will also please me

Meher Baba

"I" was the knowledge of St Francis. He adored Christ and became One with Him. Everywhere St Francis looked he could see himself; When Francis spoke it was God speaking because Francis and God were One.

This means that Francis had knowledge.

Now, how did he come by that knowledge?

He loved.

How?

He loved Christ so much he became Him.

Francis and Christ were One. More, Francis and God were One.

Why?

He adored

Why?

For Francis there was no one to love but Christ. Christ was his life. He lived for Christ.

Why?

Because Francis had spent his life searching and he sought diligently and because he sought diligently he found that which he sought.

Now Baba wants to be sought diligently. He wants us to seek him as diligently as Francis sought Jesus. Jesus forced Francis to need him. Baba wants to force us to need him.

Why?

That is the beginning of true love.

True love puts the Beloved first. Put Baba there.

Why?

It will please him.

How can we do this?

Talk to him; give him more. Tell him, 'This is what I need, so that I can try and love you as you wish me to love.'

Give him 'I' – your 'I'. 'I want', 'I have', 'I wish', 'I know' 'I think' 'I love' – don't expect him to give you these things, but do expect him to remove the desire that makes you want them.

Meher Baba is the Oversoul, the contact point of each one's awakening. Does He not say, 'it is never too late, nor is it ever too early'? It is the divine challenge, like the bell which reverberates and resounds again and again. It resounds the divine challenge of Christ, that comes to the hearing of you and I, now as it did almost 2000 years ago, and down and throughout the ages. 'Now is the acceptable time', He said. Time on earth is according to how we understand it.

The 'now' of Baba is how Baba experiences it, and Baba's statement is the divine challenge. Today we must be aroused for its fulfilment. It is the most sublime gift we can long for, or experience, and Baba is the point of contact.

> If you love me with the love Saint Frances had for Jesus, you will not only realise me, but you will also please me. - Meher Baba [*14]

'I' was the Knowledge of Saint Francis. He adored Christ and became one with Him. Everywhere Saint Francis looked he could see Himself, when Francis spoke it was God speaking because Francis and God were One. This means that Francis had Knowledge. Now how did he come by that Knowledge? He loved. How? He loved Christ so much he became Him. Francis and Christ were One. More, Francis and God were one. Why? He adored. Why? For Francis there was no one to love but Christ. Christ was his life. He lived for Christ. Why? Because Francis had spent his life searching and he sought diligently, and because he sought diligently, he found that which he sought.

Now Baba wants to be sought diligently. He wants us to seek Him as diligently as Francis sought Jesus. Jesus forced Francis to need Him. Baba wants to force us to need him. Why? That is the beginning of true love. True love puts the Beloved first. Put Baba there. Why? It will please Him.

How can we do this? Talk to Him. Give Him more. Tell Him, 'This is what I need so that I can try and love you as you wish me to love.' Give Him 'I', your 'I'. 'I want', 'I have', 'I wish', 'I know', 'I think', 'I love' - don't expect Him to remove the desire that makes you want them. Tell Him, 'When I desire You, I know You'll be pleased.' Hear Him tell you, 'When you don't desire Me, I'll be even more pleased.'

What is desire? Desire is needing. Needing is not perfection. When you no longer need even Him you will be perfect. You will see yourself everywhere, just as Saint Francis did. You will know yourself as One with Him. You will, in fact, be Him. Therefore, you cannot need Him. You will have Him, and He will have you and me, and all who have told Him 'I need You' and have searched most diligently. You will have made Him say, 'there's the one who made My most painful incarnation worthwhile'. See Him smile. Look, He stands before us with His arms wide apart to greet us when we have told Him 'I am God, I am He, and all Creation came out of Me.'

Baba – Avatar

Meher Baba is not merely Master of Perfection, He is Avatar. Why? Avatar means direct descent of God to earth in form. Which form? Our form and animal form and fish form. He is 'THE'. What does 'THE' mean? It means that in man form He is THE man. In animal form He is THE animal. In fish form He is THE fish. And so on. The word 'THE', used in this way, means that He is the one to whom everyone and everything turns. Animals will turn to THE animal, birds will turn to THE bird, fish to THE fish, and so on through all planes of consciousness. Now when man turns to THE man it will be unconsciously at first.

Baba has worked silently our way, but not in His way. Had He worked our way, had He preached and performed miracles, He would not have been heard. We are not wanting more preaching or more miracles: we have had enough. We want something far more potent. Something that will make us a little more thoughtful, something that will make us remember more.

More what? That's what we must find out. More, more, more. How can we find out more? That's where Baba comes in. How clever of Him to be silent our way when He wants us to hear Him. How beautifully He shows us silence His way, when we turn and acknowledge Him - God in Form. What a Form! How He used it. How it suffered, that lovely Form.

And when did we hear Him grumble about His suffering Form? Never. Just a little at this, 'pain in My neck' or 'the pain in My hip has fallen in love with Me!' How He suffered for us. That is the way He made us hear - He used pain. How can we grumble when we suffer when we remember THE Man suffered more than any of us ever could?

Even a Perfect Master would not suffer as THE Man suffered, for He would tell God, 'No more; this is not my function.' But suffering is the function of THE Man - Avatar. Not one of us knows how much He suffered, but we have suffered and grumbled our way until He has had to remind us: 'Come along, do it My way. It won't hurt nearly as much.'

How much more can we suffer before we turn to our Godman? How many times are we going to return to earth to suffer yet more before we realise if we do it His way, we need return no more. And what is His way? The way of suffering. To suffer His way means returning no more because we will have given him more. More what? More of ourselves, more love, more, just more. Giving Him a little more of ourselves everyday will gradually wear away all our fear, all the things we must give up before we can know Him as He really is, all our desires - our all. All of us can do that a little more for him each day our way and gradually will find ourselves giving him a little more His way.

The Prodigal

Meher Baba assures us the best study on earth for man is to study God. If we try to learn about the Master, each will learn about himself. It is what life is all about, which from beginning to end is the real purpose of our life's span on earth. In so learning it might be said, therefore, that at one time or another, one man's effort becomes more intelligent or intellectual or inspirational. He may long for God and for something more personal; still nearer, he seeks to be understood and he may yearn to experience God.

At some time, because of his prodigious living, he lets go the hold he may have of his pre-conceived ideas of God, and his former belief in any theological theories, or dry and cold intellectual formulas, or even dry and well-worn religious creeds and dogmas. In his longing for God and His truth, man is often almost driven to despair and is at his wit's end to find Him. He becomes disillusioned. He experiences in his heart the ache of unredeemed loneliness.

If, at this stage the five wits sum up the five senses and the mental faculties which have been enslaved by them, at such a helpless stage the gist of the prodigal's plight might be seen by his fellow human beings as a just recompense. Such is the working out of the KARMIC law which Meher Baba defines as being inexorable in its working.

The law, however, which is above it is the divine law of Love. It is God's gift to humanity and is brought to earth where it is 'bottled up' in the divine form and person of the Ancient One, Avatar or Messiah, or the Christ whose name today is Meher Baba.

Love divine, all love excelling,
Joy of heaven to earth come down. [*15]

---❣❣❣ ---

Love divine - all love excelling
joy of heaven to earth come down Hymn.

Time and Timelessness

There have been many instances when the Master would call a meeting at which certain devotees were to be present. I have in mind one meeting when He had some specific spiritual work He was about to carry out, the nature and impart of which was known to Him alone. To facilitate certain aspects of the work He would call for volunteers from among the devotees present, having defined the ability required and the task which each would be required to carry out faithfully and, one might add, unfailingly.

One task recorded elsewhere was when He required a specified number of devotees (I believe it was six) to each sit in a chair and remain awake throughout twenty-four hours. When volunteers were told to raise their hand, several hands were raised, and some hesitatingly. Out of the number, Baba chose the six required as deftly as He handled His alphabet board, and as if He had pre-knowledge of each one's ability to carry out the task. The reader may then say: If Baba already knew, why does He go through these preliminary arrangements? There may of course be many reasons, but I offer my thoughts on this.

Baba draws people to Him from all over the globe out of their love alone for Him. The spiritual status of Meher Baba has been defined in spiritual terms, names, and definitions in the minutest detail in the book *God Speaks*, along the lines of intellectual and scientific terms, spiritual states and qualities. However, Meher Baba is best understood through the Love which he awakens in the heart and soul of the human being. There is of course 'best', 'better' and 'very best' which are terms which might be further expounded on, appropriately repeatedly to appease the mind, but Meher Baba would still be beyond the ken of human understanding. According to Baba, Love is the answer, Love is the remedy. Did not Jesus in a similar way convey the same meaning when He said: My grace is sufficient for you, for my power is made perfect in weakness?[*16]

Again, to that question, how many of us would be drawn to Him if Baba, in His timeless state, did not conform also to time as we understand time? Whilst being Divine, Baba is also human, and whilst He is all-knowing, He appears as though He does not know. He has come down to our level and He becomes one with us on all levels of consciousness but is not bound by it. He is Universal in consciousness and, for the spiritual purpose of the upliftment of Humanity, He works on all levels.

At such a time, after hours of spiritual discourses and explanations to satisfy the intellectual approach to the subject by those present, he would pause and ask as to whether he should continue. Then he would say 'the majority have it' - and so he continued. Sometimes he would explain at great length a discourse which is to be understood as the function of the heart, and he would define to the utmost detail the importance of such spiritual aspects concerning Love - human and divine.

Whilst being with us, He was also one of us on every level. In reminding us that He was our friend, this also implied that we were to be candid and honest. At such a time, after hours of spiritual discourses and explanations to satisfy the intellectual approach to the subject by those present, He would pause and ask whether He should continue. Then He would say, "The majority have it" and so He continued. Sometimes He would explain at great length a discourse which is to be understood as the function of the heart, and He would define to the utmost detail the importance of such spiritual aspects concerning Love - human and divine.

It was evident that whatever the import or signification touching on any aspect of Truth, Baba was always in command of the whole situation. Explanations on various themes were received, not as differing facets of Truth, but one's conviction that Meher Baba is Himself Truth incarnate in this twentieth century was apparent as He expounded upon different aspects of the whole panorama. Words have their limitations and with all the words at His disposal, we humans may even so fail to grasp the import of the underlying spiritual meaning of some of His explanations, and thus the mind with its limitations could hardly if ever be satisfied. This fact became quite clear to one's understanding. The complete human being is he whose heart and mind have become balanced, the heart for feelings, and the mind for discrimination. This is the outcome of spiritual understanding which is above rules.

His explanations made me more conscious and aware of my own failings. Often, He Himself would tend to become more personal towards us, like an all-loving father giving advice to His children, and His assurances were at all times enhanced by His deep humility. In approaching Him as the Highest of the High, the imponderables of the human mind somehow became sublimated as never before so that the finer intuitions served the needs of one's innermost heart.

The Resources of Humanity are Finite

All the might, power and strength of mankind are finite. What then avails, since they are ineffectual for redeeming the loneliness of the human heart, and for the renewal of the human mind?

The divine challenge comes as the only reality, the rallying force and play which can operate singularly within, independently of the illusory universe, and help us to discriminate between the real and the false values which confront the human being daily during his or her life.

Talents and Abilities

When you vouchsafe your talents to Baba, using them to the utmost efficiency, they become True Love's offering and sacrifice. And when the diversity of abilities is gradually streamlined throughout the aspirant's life, they tend to converge at one point. But all along the devotee must find his or her own way of loving the Beloved. That which motivates towards the highest good is the ideal watchword. Through abilities one can use them creatively, harmoniously and with enthusiasm. When devotion takes a lead, it becomes a means by which it may wing its way into hearts and minds, unknown but to God. Like rays of light which meet and are focused on one point, so the mind is no longer scattered. The one-track mind can express higher powers of impassioned feeling and imagination to bring to bear upon the beautiful, as in a poem that portrays an imaginative picture and expresses in words something between the ardent lover and the Beloved.

The mysticism which powerfully stirs the imagination is the offering of the self-surrendered lover who has manipulated all the puppets of his own life in True Love's offering to the Beloved, and attains by grace to direct spiritual heights in communion and in adoration of the Beloved.

Spiritual History Repeats Itself

Spiritual history, in depicting the life of the spirit, repeats itself and emerges in its glory and beatitude partly revealed in the life of Lord Zoroaster during His short Avatarhood. The revelation becomes meaningful and aptly sets forth a glimpse of the divine qualities of Baba's incarnation.

> Undimmed by the flow of time its essence immerges into the light of the present and beyond, and becomes ignited and characterized in the divinity of the Lord and Saviour Meher Baba.

Undimmed by the flow of time, its essence emerges into the light of the present and beyond and becomes ignited and characterized in the divinity of the Lord and Saviour Meher Baba.

Little is known of Zoroaster, founder of the Zoroastrian religion. It was, however, the religion of Merwan's family, for they were Parsee. Similarly, the youth of Jesus was associated with the religion of his family, which happened to be the Jewish faith.

Since Baba is the essence and the Truth of all religions, He has stated that He belongs to none and that all religions belong to Him. They echo down the ages the muffled call to

Humanity to prepare themselves for their deliverance. Beams of light emerge from their essence into the present like silent prophets whose message becomes lost to the clamouring din of humanity.

At each succeeding close of the old and the beginning of a new cycle, they herald the coming of the Saviour on earth into incarnation once again.

The 'Now'

The past is in the present, and the future is in the present, as the 'NOW' of Baba. He said many things would come to light. The true authenticity of spiritual history must of course depend upon Him, since much of what the Avatar has taught in past cycles is not available, because the human mind has lost its grip on the subtlety of the spiritual meaning in the teaching. There is little known regarding the youth of Zoroaster, founder of the Zoroastrian religion, and so the writer relates that which has become legendary.

The Prophet Daniel, who is reputed to have been His master, declared Zoroaster's status as Avatar, and in so doing the Prophet sang the following hymn of praise. In its mystical meaning, there is a close association which characterises the mission of the Avatars Zoroaster and Jesus, as indeed the meaning becomes also vivid in Baba as Avatar in the present.

<u>The 'NOW'</u>

The past is in the present, and the future is in the present, as the 'now' of Baba. He said many things would come to light, The true authenticity of spiritual history must of course depend upon Him, since much of what the avatar has taught in past cycles is not available because the human mind has lost grip on the subtlety of the spiritual meaning in the teaching.

There is little known regarding the youth of Zoroaster, founder of the Parsee religion, and so the writer relates that which has become legendary.

The prophet Daniel, who is reputed to have been his master declared Zoroaster's status as avatar and in so doing the prophet sang the following hymn of praise.

In its mystical meaning there is a close association which characterizes the mission of the avatar Zoroaster and Jesus as indeed the meaning becomes also vivid in Baba as avatar in the present.

---

*

The Hymn of Daniel to Zoroaster – translated from Avestan language[*17]:

Behold the voice of the ages is in me, the earth departeth and the glory of the Lord cometh – He cometh quickly. In His right hand are the ages, and the days and nights are under His feet. The stars of heaven tremble. The arch of the outer firmament is shivered like a broken bow, and the curtain of the sky is rent in pieces as a veil in the tempest. The sun and the moon shriek aloud, and the ocean becomes an uproar before the Lord.

The nations are extinct as the ashes of a fire that has gone out, and the kings of the earth are no more. He hath bruised the earth in a mortar, and the dust of it is scattered abroad in the heavens. The stars in their might He hath pounded to pieces, and the foundations of the ages to fine powder. But out of the north arises a fair glory with brightness, and the breath of the Lord breathes life into all things. The beam of the dawn is risen, and there shall be times and seasons again, and the Being of the majesty of God is made manifest in form. From the dust of the earth is the earth made again, and of the beams of His glory shall He make new stars. Praise the Lord in whom is Life, and in whom all things have Being! Praise Him and glorify Him that is risen with the wings of the morning heaven; in whose breath the stars breathe, in whose brightness the firmament is lightened! Praise Him who maketh the wheels of the sphere run their course. Praise Him winter and summer. Praise Him stars of heaven. Praise Him men and women of the earth! Praise and glory and honour be unto the Highest, who sits upon the Throne for ever, and ever.

A song reputed to be of ancient origin is said to have been recalled by one of Zoroaster's lovers at that time during

His temporary absence and sung in anticipation of His return. It is versified in the following:

> My ear in the darkness listens for the sound of His coming. My eyes watch for Him and rest not, for I would not He found me sleeping. For when my Beloved cometh, He is like the beam in the morning. Even as the dawn in a strange land to the sight of a man journeying. Yes, when my Beloved cometh, as dew that descends from heaven, no man can hear when it falleth, but as rain it refreshes all things. The night-winds make sweet songs for Him, even in the darkness, soft music. Wherever he goes, there His sweetness goes before Him.

The hymns of praise, adoration and glorification ever dedicated in the past, to either one Avatar or another, from one cycle to another, are the praiseworthy attributes of Baba in their essence, either manifest or unmanifest in Him in our time. At the time of His manifestation, Christians will see him as Christ and become spiritually awakened and know Baba as Christ. Truth, and its essence is not divided at any time nor is it because of the divine forms through which it has been made presentable to humanity in past cycles. It is One, Indivisible and Universal, throughout time and eternity.

*

The Eternal Divine Now

The eternal divine NOW

When Christ told His listeners, 'Now is the acceptable time', that moment is explained by Baba —

The past is in the present and the future is in the past, and the past and the future are in the the NOW.

He says, It is never too late and it is never too early. The 'Now' of Christ is the 'Now' of Baba.

When Christ told His disciples, 'Now is the acceptable time', that moment is explained by Baba thus. The past is in the present and the future is in the past, and the past and the future are in the 'now'. He says, it is never too late, and it is never too early. The 'now' of Christ is the 'now' of Baba.

It is the answer to the assumption that the Ancient One, who seemingly had held Himself aloof from His creatures, descends from His exalted state to be one amongst us. So, it can be seen in these fragments, which were in part the essence of the Zoroastrian faith, becoming most meaningfully ignited by the light of Baba's divinity, and characterised once again in His divine attributes while in our midst.

The Apostolic mission of Saint Francis of Assisi was also

characterised in his prayers of praise and adoration, giving thanks to God intoned with a call to all men to awaken:

'So be it Lord, Thy throne shall never
Like earth's proud empires, pass away.
Thy Kingdom stands, and grows forever,
Till all thy creatures own thy sway.[*18]

Meher Baba's Tomb

Baba's tomb at Meherabad, India is situated on the crest of a hill outlined by the sky. The area is hallowed for miles around, and the vaulted heavens, and the soil of earth, meet amidst the small cluster of huts and out-houses. The four walls of the tomb are surmounted at each corner of the domed roof by a symbol for each of four of the five great religions of the world. On the western corner is a cross[*19] for Christianity and spaced at the other three corners are a crescent moon for Islam, a fire-bowl for Zoroastrianism, and a temple for Hinduism.

The Tomb symbolises the 'container' for Church, Mosque, Fire-temple, and Temple, whilst Baba is the living and eternal essence within them all, which men seek the world over.*20

Baba is the Saviour to be found and experienced in the awakening of the heart. Above the door at the entrance to the Tomb is the inscription of Baba's motto, 'Mastery in Servitude.' It stands for sacrifice of rest and easement for the benefit of Love and Service to Humanity.

NOTE   In Matt: 21 Verse 42: appears the following quotation. –

'Jesus saith unto them, did ye never read in the scriptures, the stone which the builders rejected, the same is become the head of the corner: This is the Lord's doing, and it is marvellous in our eyes*(the eyes of the family)

* The scriptures Jesus was referring to is in chapt. 29 verse 16, Isaiah the Prophet of the Old Testament.

♦ 'Our eyes' (the eyes Divine) Read Baba's Prayer (Parvardigar) dictated by Baba Sept. 1959, in which it says: 'you are indivisible, and none can see you, but with eyes Divine'.

Everyone is Extremely Important but not all are Equal

From Baba comes to this age of humanity the simple answer to this 20th Century riddle. Whether it be a world leader or the 'untouchable', the chasm created by man through ignorance becomes explicit in the understanding of Baba's explanations and teaching. Where the thought, word or action arises it becomes expedient in practise and understanding to exercise brotherly or sisterly feeling towards each other one as the occasion presents itself, remembering that a man or woman is more than a person. Each one is a soul. They are not as they think themselves to be.

In thinking and behaviour, each believes himself a separate human being, whereas in fact he is not as he believes, even a separate soul. It is all within the realm of false thinking. It is through the emanation of Baba we are told that all Souls are one. He has explicitly stated – 'Not we, but One', and 'One Is'. Because there is much superficial thinking prevalent in the world, it is imperative for the Baba lover to recognise and cherish the extreme importance of each and every one, without ignoring the apparently innumerable divisions which separate man from man, and by which he may be constantly bewildered.

It is here that the powerful, the famous, the world leaders or whatever happens to be the worldly status of the individual, the weak or the strong, the rich or the poor, the good or the bad, that each one is infinitely important as soul. At every point the mundane life of man is categorised by status or authority. Though considered to be necessary, it is neither absolute nor permanent. The inhabitants of the earth are individually important. This becomes a point to be understood at different levels.

When the writer was in Baba's company, as in this

instance of a mass Darshan when scores of thousands of people gathered from distant parts of India to receive his Prasad or blessing, there were also present with Him on the raised dais, men with public authority who had come both to pay their respects and proclaim their acknowledgement of Baba over the microphone. Then proceeded in full swing a living stream of humanity, impatiently moving forward and becoming like a torrential river as it approached the Ocean to be absorbed into it.

60,000 or more men, women and children pressed forward to where Baba was seated on the dais. As the vast crowd formed into a single file column, and as every individual arrived at the feet of the Beloved, separation became resolved as each became as one drop returning to the Ocean for a timeless moment of the divinized substance of God. At brief intervals Baba had short messages given out over the microphone appropriate for the occasion and touching upon the life of the spirit. The gestures of Baba at the arriving and departing of each devotee evidently conveyed something much deeper than the surface scene. The mass darshan continued hour after hour. One of the Mandali suggested to Baba that He should have a rest, to which He replied: "This is My rest!"

*

The Swan and the Sparrow

When the swan takes flight it has one purpose, and with outstretched neck fixed towards reaching its destination, it takes the shortest and most direct line towards any place or object.

The sparrow flits about from tree to tree, with an eye on morsels. He is a creature which delays. It often makes him prey for the owl or the hawk. But Jesus drew attention to the sparrow, telling his disciples that:

> 'What is the price of two sparrows – one copper coin? But not a single sparrow can fall to the ground without your Father knowing it. [*21] Not even a sparrow falleth to the ground but is known of by God the Father.'

Similarly, Baba declared that not a leaf could quiver except by His wish.

Although both swan and sparrow differ in their natures, are not both alike in importance in the sight of God? Do not our natures also vary? They vary according to each man and woman, and Baba declares to us that each one is extremely important.

Whereas man can overcome his own nature through Baba's grace, the sparrow and swan cannot. To man is given the choice. The choice of what? To choose whether he will pander to his lower nature or serve his higher nature. Our 'will' becomes free when we make it Baba's 'will'. Of course, we can choose.

You ask someone for a ballpoint pen. They offer you one by holding out two pens of different colours. You are not offered both, so you make your choice. Is that not free will? Baba gives us the choice. In making all 'will' Baba's 'will', it is an act of True Love at the altar of sacrifice. Any man or woman can do it.

> 'I am the Ancient One. Not a leaf has the power to quiver without My wish. I am the One who knows everything about everyone. I am Krishna, I am Buddha, I am Christ' - Meher Baba [*22]

The Flash

The 'Flash' comes as the transiency by which the mind retains a moment of divine knowledge. It comes as a gift. Whatever is received in the Flash remains with the aspirant and is some aspect and attribute of divinity allied in character and properties and understood through spiritual understanding.

It surpasses a lifetime of accumulated intellectual knowledge and can be expounded in intellectual terms or through mysticism, but the Flash is revelation which bears the stamp of unmistakable divine authority and since it is a gift of the divine, it surpasses all earthly confines and transcends the lucidity and clarity, knowledge or understanding, which the mind of itself can achieve. It is not for the asking and comes instantaneously, unexpectedly, and at the right time.

The Flash

The flash comes as the transient by which the mind retains a moment of divine knowledge. It comes as a gift. Whatever is received in the flash remains with the aspirant, and is some aspect and attribute of divinity, allied in character and properties and understood through spiritual understanding.

It surpasses a life time of accumulated intellectual knowledge and can be expounded in intellectual terms or through mysticism, but the flash is revelation which bears the stamp of unmistakable divine authority, and since it is a gift of the divine it surpasses all earthly confines and transcends the lucidity and clarity, knowledge or understanding which the mind of itself can achieve.

It is not for the asking and comes instantaneously, unexpected and at the right time.

It is received in reverential wonder and remains with the aspirant as permanent spiritual knowledge and subsides all doubts.

From earthbound speculation it lifts one into the realms of silent inner adoration of God as an aspect of the divine.

The Flash is received in reverential wonder and remains with the aspirant as permanent spiritual knowledge and subsides all doubts. From earthbound speculation it lifts one into the realms of silent inner adoration of God as an aspect of the Divine.

The teachings of Meher Baba come to fruition during the

awakening process of the aspirant and of which he may not always be aware. Awakening comes about through the Master's grace. His teachings enable the aspirant to identify his own limited and inherent nature and its age-long bearing upon his own characteristics and varying shades of the ingredients of the good or bad. He becomes convinced of the truth which Baba brings to humanity. He further becomes convicted when his heart and mind become no longer at loggerheads, and when the mind becomes submissive to the heart. It is an adjustment between the two which restrains and transforms the persistent and aggressive ego.

Baba is the source of infinite knowledge and bliss. The aspirant derives a clear apprehension of truth or fact through actual cognition and inner experience, for Baba has consummate knowledge and understanding of an individual. The outcome is such that the aspirant becomes gradually freed from the ingredients of an impure life, which in turn urges him to press forward. He also becomes possessed of a living and dynamic faith.

'I am the Divine Beloved who loves you more than you can ever love yourself.'*24

———— ♡ ————

I love you more than you can ever love yourself. —

Meher Baba

———— ♡ ————

Fred's Conclusion to *Experiences*

The reader will gather in, and conclude for himself, either from reasoning or by an appeal to his Higher Self. Since the air man breathes is a gift from God, infinitely more potent is the Grace of God, which is the redemption or salvation of man's soul. From among the fragments that are related, one may infer a conclusion - which on the other hand may be the beginning!

o—o—o—O—o—o—o

I have deemed it my good portion to have been born poor
of this world's fortune —
Yet, in this fate of 'ups and downs' I played the ace of
Baba's clowns
And found no mirth in the Kingdom of Earth, but now I know
That I am Thine, God's Kingdom's come and Thou art mine.

o—o—o—O—o—o—o

Fred Marble,
25 Oct. 1965.

Part Three

Appendices:

1. Contacts with Meher Baba's Mandali
2. English Arti and Creative Writing
3. Obituary
4. Epilogue

Appendix 1 - Contacts with Meher Baba's Mandali

Our Friend is with us,
wherefore then should we seek more than this?
The treasure of His converse is to our fond hearts sufficient bliss.

We will never know the full extent of Fred's contact with Baba's Mandali, but a comprehensive collection of letters was 'saved' from Fred's home after his passing, and Keith Miles has lovingly shared them for the purposes of this book. Requests to view them can be made via *mbaboard@yahoo.com*.

Fred first wrote to Beloved Baba in the mid-forties. Sometimes his letters were answered by Adi Snr. and in later years by Baba's sister Mani. I cannot include all the correspondence with India between the pages of this book but have selected some that not only reflect Fred's on-going contact with Baba's Mandali, but also reveal something of the personalities of each one, and how Fred interacted with them. Messages from Baba have been included in foregoing chapters.

Beloved Baba's Mehera

Mehera was Baba's Chief Woman Disciple of whom He famously said, "She is My very breath without which I cannot live."

Christmas 1983

Baba's very dear Fred,

May you have a Merry Mehermas and Joyous New Year '83 filled with Baba's love. We were all so happy that Baba gave you the strength to come here this time to His Home again. May you have the strength and love to come closer and closer to your Beloved so that He is always with you. With love in Beloved Baba from all your Meherazad family.

In His all-embracing love,

Mehera

*

August 1984

Dear Fred,

A loving Jai Meher Baba to you from all Meherazad family. I received the bottle of 'Complan' you sent and deeply appreciate your loving thought and concern on my behalf.

By Beloved Baba's grace the collar bone has mended well, and I am using my arm again quite normally. During those first weeks of pain, I thought of Beloved Baba all the more and the physical suffering and hardships He had undergone for the sake of the world and felt He had given me a tiny share of it.

We played the tape of the arti composed for the Beloved that very evening in the drawing room where we often sat in the evenings with Beloved Baba, and He would ask for His favourite qawwali records to be played, and I felt Beloved Baba was with us listening to the arti. It is truly a beautiful composition coming from your heart expressing your love for Beloved Baba. As Lol Benbow's voice is soft, the music could have been softer for the words to be heard clearly by everyone.

I am enclosing a locket of Beloved Baba for you. Be happy in Baba's love - know that He is always with you and loves you.

With a loving Jai Baba from all your Meherazad family.

In His love, Mehera

Baba's sister Mani

Through her deepest desire, Mani was allowed to join Baba and the women Mandali when she left school in 1932. She became Mehera's protector and constant companion and later served as Chairman of the Trust.

More than twenty letters or notes were found from Mani spanning 1958-1982, some quite personal, others acknowledging the donations Fred sent to the Trust, where Mani would often add a brief greeting. I include the special ones. To give context to Mani's first letter, I include an extract from Fred's journal. He writes:

A letter was received at 'Meher Manzil'[*1] stating Baba required some early issues of a favourite boy's publication – a weekly circulation during the pre-war period. The paper took the form of a comic weekly, it was called the *Union Jack,* with small, coloured picture illustrations depicting exciting deeds of daring and was very popular at the time with schoolboys and read by adults in moments of leisure. Coming across these items presented a difficulty because they had not been heard of for years. A private collector came to my notice whereupon inquiries bought a reply that a few editions were available and surprisingly in mint condition. They were immediately purchased and sent to 'Mannie.' *[Fred's spelling]* Baba found relaxation through such items.

Another item wanted was for Mehera, it was a book with the title *Captain Donald the Duck*! This puzzled me because I imagined *Captain Donald* might be a ship's captain or, that *Captain Donald* might be a creature of the farmyard. I found a number of book publishers and invariably the reply was short and curious. They had never heard of it. In any case it would be out of print. Moreover, I suspected they thought I was joking. Then one day I noticed some books for sale on a table in the forefront of a Putney church gateway and there was the book, *Captain Donald the Duck*.

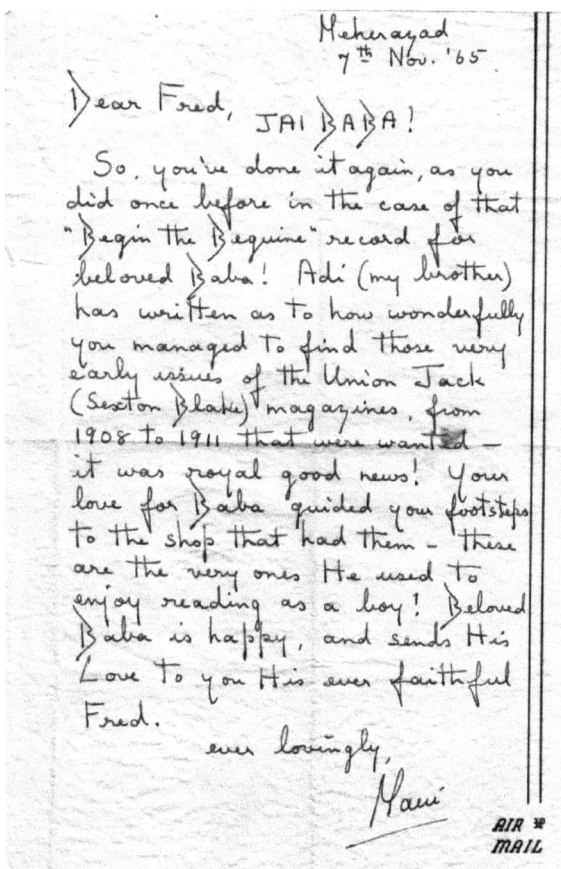

7th Nov 1965, Meherazad – Mani writes:

Dear Fred, Jai Baba!

So, you've done it again as you did once before in the case of that *Begin the Beguine* record for Beloved Baba. Adi, my brother, has written as to how wonderfully you managed to find those very early issues of the *Union Jack'* (Sexton Blake) magazines from 1908 to 1911 that were wanted. It was Royal good news! Your love for Baba guided your footsteps to the shop that had them. These are the very ones He used to enjoy reading as a boy. Beloved Baba is happy and sends his love to you, His ever-faithful Fred.

Ever lovingly, Mani

*

Fred was never forgotten by his family in Meherazad, and this touching note was received from Mani possibly in acknowledgement of a pending health procedure.

Dear, dear Fred,

Jai Baba from us all. You will be specially remembered on 3 April – Beloved Baba will be with you, holding your hand all the time. We love you and call out with you:

AVATAR MEHER BABA KI JAI - Mani

And the letters continued through the seventies back and forth, and often referenced Fred's involvement and care for Adi, Franey and Shireen, Mani often thanking Fred for his help and support. So, we know he fulfilled Baba's request despite his own advancing years and his frailty that was noted by those who met him then. How encouraging these contacts from Mani must have been in those days. One little donation receipt carrying a hastily penned note from her reads:

> When dear Franee[*2] was here she lovingly mentioned what a 'faithful friend' you are to the Meher Manzil family. It is all Beloved Baba's Grace. Our thoughts fly many a time to Baba's very dear Fred, and we hope this finds you in good health and Baba cheer. Beloved Baba is always with you. Love from us all, in Him, your sister, Mani.

And who wouldn't want to be considered Mani's sister?

The following seems to have been prompted by Fred's frequent donations to the Trust:

> 16th November 1981
>
> Dear Fred,
>
> Another opportunity from Beloved Baba to send greetings to His dear Fred. We are most touched by

your heart's unfailing remembrance, but I do hope you are being practical dear Fred and not neglecting your own needs when donating to the Trust. Baba would want his Fred well cared for too! Happy to know that Franee, Jay and Shireen plan to visit you, perhaps by now they have already been. Of course, dear Adi's health keeps Franee so occupied, but visiting you is a real family outing. And I am sure by Baba's grace our Delia will have a favourable report of the investigation. Yes, Beloved Baba has his loving attention on all, in turns.

Your 'aches and pains' epistle seem but an extension of what is happening here! It is all His blessings which we recognise much later when the disguise is off.

Much love from us all dear Fred, and also to Lol Benbow when you see him. Avatar Meher Baba Ki Jai!

Mani

***

There now follow some examples of correspondence with other members of Baba's women Mandali. They require little comment.

Khorshed Irani

Khorshed was one of Baba's earliest women disciples who, aged 13, was introduced by Baba to Mehera, and they became best of friends. She spent the closing years of her life in Kushroo Quarters in Ahmednagar where, certainly, Fred would have made her acquaintance.

2nd September 1984

Dear Friend Fred Marks, Jai Baba.

Hope this will find you in best of health and happy. I received the bottle of orange marmalade. Thank you very much. I enjoyed it very much. Sudam and Asha have second daughter born on 18 August '84. She is nice. By Baba's Grace we are fine. Hope same is with you. Jai Baba, Khorshed, Sudam, Asha[*3].

***

Mansari Desai

Mansari was instructed by Baba before He embarked on the New Life to stay in Meherabad and caretake His Samadhi. This she did lovingly, greeting pilgrims from around the world and delighting them with Baba stories, and lemonade, in her kitchen, until her passing in 1997. The familiarity of her greeting to Fred typifies her most natural, playful, and loving nature that all who met her experienced. When asked *[by the Editor]* how she had 'endured' never being able to leave the Hill she replied, "what need have I to leave when the whole world comes to visit?"

Meherabad, 6th September 1984

Darling Fred kiddo – Beloved Baba, Jai Baba!

Knew about you sweet one from our Rosemary and felt happy. Big candles light little ones! Jai Baba Fredji, so nice of you to send me 'honey ginger' bottle; I have it in my milk at night. So considerate of you, but please do not trouble; it reminds me of my favourite lines:

'Little deeds of kindness, little words of love, makes this earth a heaven, like the heaven above.'*4

It makes me happy because it comes from Baba's Fred. Live long Fred, that you may spread 'Baba' in your way – that affects the heart more. Keep fit for His work. So? Wish you the best in Baba – yours in Baba, Mansari's Jai, Jai Baba!

*

And another from Mansari:

Fredji, your beautiful Arti we read and sent it to our Bob Brown to set it in a befitting way of melody. It is Beloved's Gift to you. We heard it on the recorder. Words are just right. Because He is the Right! Go on doing that Fred.

Jai Baba – Mansari's hug. Keep happy in Baba to make others happy. Jai Jai BABA.

***

Rano Gayley

Rano was an American artist who met Baba in 1933 and became His disciple, living much of her life with the women Mandali in India and executing many paintings on spiritual themes under Baba's direction.

Ahmednagar, 2nd April 1979

Dear Fred,

Mani is away for some days on holiday – so I am acknowledging your loving gift to Beloved Baba's Trust.

I am sorry to hear that Adi is not improving – I will keep your letter and give it to Mani on her return which will be around the 15th April. I hope you are keeping well. Beloved Baba is always with you.

In His love, Rano

***

Delia DeLeon

Delia, a native of Panama who founded the Q Theatre in Richmond, met Baba in 1931 and instantly recognised Him as her Beloved. She travelled with Baba in India and Europe and was instrumental in founding the first UK Baba group, Meher Universal Spiritual League. She was central in welcoming the new wave of young Baba lovers who came in the '60s. The few letters between Fred and Delia mostly concerned plans for Baba meetings, but since they met frequently they had little need to write. I include this brief one which seems profound retrospectively, in recording the arrival of *God Speaks* on UK shores. What a 'bargain' *God Speaks* was back then!

My dear Fred,

The Committee accept your offer of the Hall for September 27th. Allan Cohen[*5] will be coming over so it will fit in very well. 'God Speaks' is now available so will you send a cheque to the U.S. League. It is £2 plus 2 shillings postage.

Yours Delia

***

Kitty Davy

Kitty was a contemporary of Delia DeLeon and one of Baba's first hosts in the UK in the '30s. Thereafter she joined Him in India and on travels through Europe. In 1952, during a visit to Myrtle Beach, Baba directed her to stay and help Elizabeth Patterson run the Meher Spiritual Center, where she remained till her passing.

The following single letter demonstrates most perfectly Kitty's characteristically forthright manner and her utter clarity. One wonders how it was received by Fred who was trying to donate books to the Center Library!

26th January 1966

Dear Fred.

Quick note to let you know the parcel of books arrived here safely. Some I found interesting but not all, for example 'Hafiz in London' has no connection with Hafiz the poet, nor has 'Rose-in-Hood' which is not Hafiz at all. Did you look into, or read either yourself? Neither I nor Elizabeth cared for either. Frances Havegal's poems are not much read today as are not Tennyson – but as you say the one *Take My Life,* Baba has made important to us all. The *Milarepa* is not as interesting as the one I already have of his in the library, but it may grow on one.

Anyway, this criticism in no way reflects on the kindness and work you must have given to tracing even these. Watkins[*6] has an addition which I think better than the *Odes* - but we have two copies already of Watkins. So, we will place all in our library save two I am returning in the hopes that you can exchange maybe for the *Christian Mystics*. I see the two copies of *Odes* are identical that you sent - no difference in content - but I will hold onto those. The two I am returning are *Hafiz in London* and *Rose-in-Hood*.

Now I have the *Awakeners* ready done up to send I'm only awaiting word from Filis. I note the other issues you would like, and we'll see what can be done. Thank you for copy of cable re Anne Powell's demise. I'm happy for her people that Baba sent it. Next event 'Baba's Birthday'. Did I tell you of a message to someone here that if we wholeheartedly loved Baba and had faith in Him that soon after November 27, 1967, by Baba's Grace we would know who He really was? Two years seems a long time, but not really. No time for more - thank you once again for your interest and trouble taken which I do appreciate.

In Baba's love Kitty

***

Fred also had contact with Baba's men Mandali:

Adi Junior

Adi was the youngest of Baba's brothers, sent to live in England after his marriage to Franey and directed to work with Fred. While working together, there was seldom the need to correspond, so only a handful of letters from Adi, and his daughter Shireen remain, the latter thanking 'Uncle Fred' for gifts. I include these from Adi to give a flavour of their relationship.

10 Feb 1961

Dear Fred,

I must ask you to forgive me for not answering your last letter earlier, but at that time I was suffering from a bad cold which unfortunately recently developed into influenza, and I have been in bed for a few days. It is only today that I'm feeling a little better and I'm able to answer letters.

We were all sorry to hear about your illness and do hope you have got over it now. It must be very difficult when you were entirely on your own and cannot let anyone know in case of sudden illness. I wish you were on the telephone so we could be in more frequent contact with each other - though I need hardly tell you we are always close together in spirit. Freni and I would be very happy if you could visit us one Saturday or Sunday whenever it suits you and 'break Baba's bread' with us.

With loving regards in Baba from all at *Meher Manzil*, Adi

*

7th August 1969, *Meher Manzil*

Dear Fred,

Thank you for your letter of the 5th. I only hope that in our rightful enthusiasm for making outer contacts, we do not lose sight of the supreme importance of maintaining and increasing our 'inner contact' with Baba, by continuing to carry out, side by side, to the best of our ability the instructions He so clearly and definitely gave us regarding business. It would be a tragic mistake for anyone to think that because Baba dropped His body, the instructions, and orders He gave us are no longer necessary - that would not only be a mockery of the work we think we are doing for Him, it would be a denial of His Eternal Divinity.

I agree that the good weather should be taken advantage of for travelling (for those who can afford it) and contacting people. I do expect and hope, however, that although business seems to be rather slack at the moment, we should maintain contact with each other at regular, and not too infrequent, intervals.

In Baba's love from all at *Meher Manzil,* Adi.

***

Adi K Irani

Adi was an early disciple from the Manzil-e-Meem days and who later served for many years as Baba's Secretary, living in Ahmednagar. Fred first corresponded with Adi in 1946, and this continued until 1976. Adi was charged with sending potent messages from Beloved Baba to Western lovers.

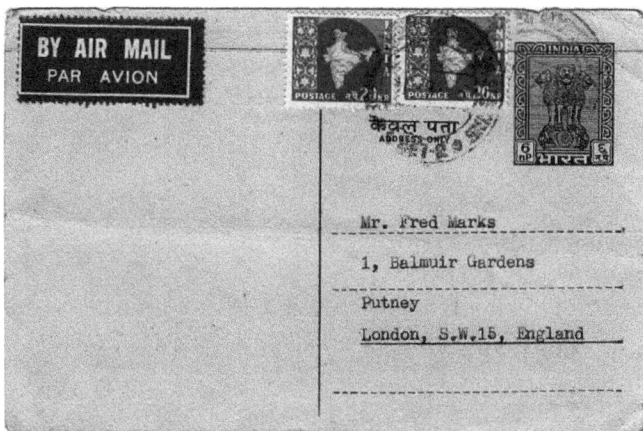

GOD MAN
BY C. B. PURDOM
Rs. 30-00. Postage. Rs 2·00

ADI K. IRANI
SECRETARY
AVATAR MEHER BABA
King's Road, Ahmednagar

GOD SPEAKS
BY AVATAR MEHER BABA
Rs. 30-00. Postage Rs. 2-00

My dear Fred,   Sept.11, 1965

I acknowledge with thanks your letter of 6th, but by now you will have come to know of the decision of beloved Baba not to hold the Western Sahavas next December.

I am sure that you will remain happy to abide by His wish.

With loving regards,

Yours as ever

*

King's Road, Ahmednagar, September 11th, 1965

My dear Fred,

I acknowledge with thanks your letter of 6th; I know you will have come to know of the decision of Beloved Baba not to hold the Western Sahavas next December.

I am sure that you will remain happy to abide by His wish. With loving regards, yours as ever, Adi.

Adi also arranged translations into Hindi and Telegu of articles Fred sent to him, and both printed and distributed them to various groups, and sent them to the Editors of *Divya*

Vani. Evidently Fred dispatched postal orders to cover costs incurred.

Ahmednagar, India. March 14, 1966

My dear Fred,

Pardon me for very late acknowledgment of your letter of March 3rd along with two typed copies of your beautiful small article *Reminiscences of Meher Baba.*

I noted that you sent one copy to the *Awakener,* and the 2 copies I received are sent by me today to the editors of *Meher Pukar*, Hindi and *Avatar Meher,* Telugu, for publication in their respective magazines.

Glory be to all your love for Baba!

With loving regards, yours ever,

Adi.

And so, letters continued through the '60s and '70s, the last concerning a proposed visit by Fred to Meherabad in which Adi outlines, as he must have done for countless pilgrims over decades, where to go, with whom to stay in Mumbai and Nagar, all with exacting detail and loving service. When Jack Small, an American Baba lover, came to volunteer with Adi, notable 'additions' to the letters appeared such as: 'bring Elastoplast' or 'so and so needs Sellotape', and thus the integration of East and West continued to unfold.

***

Jal Irani

Jal, another of Baba's younger brothers, lived in the family home in Poona. Unsurprisingly, Fred had over fifty letters from Jal since Jal was a prolific writer. The phrase 'social networker' might also apply. He greeted most of Baba's lovers coming from the West. Correspondence between Jal and Fred began after the East-West Gathering in 1962 and continued until November 1976. The letters mostly referenced Fred's regular gifts of postal orders or cheques, and amply illustrate Fred's generosity and the loving fellowship in which he held Jal. For brevity I include just two.

6 January 1963

My Dearest brother Fred,

I wish you a very happy and joyous New Year. I hope sincerely that by the grace and utmost love of our Beloved Baba you are well and happy - how I miss you so much Fred. At times I go near Napier

Hotel and feel your absence then go back so sad and lonely. How I wish I'd stayed with you much longer with Beloved Baba. But you've gone far away after being only for a short time with us. But I pray that by Baba's grace and love we meet again soon together with Beloved Baba and stay for a long time. Amen. Your immense love and sacrifice for dear Baba has really made me so proud of you.

You are my dearest loving brother you are so kind and generous. I worship you in my heart forever as my dearest real brother. How are you there, dearest friend? Please take care of your health as this year fog and cold was very severe in London. How I miss you. Do write to me whenever you feel like, any news of Baba and yourself dear.

How can I forget your immense love for Baba. We belong to each other as dearest brothers of Baba since ages. Baba the Ancient One, how can I forget you and your kindness dear Fred. Write to me once in a while dear Fred. How are you there getting on? My deepest love and remembrance to you my dearest brother Fred. Also convey my sincere love and remembrance to all dearest lovers of beloved Baba, will you? Thanks, as we all belong to Baba family as real sisters and brothers from ages with Beloved Baba - the Ancient One. I hope to meet you soon again and be with Baba by his Grace and love and stay together for a longer time my dearest loving brother Fred.

Jal

PS You are the most and kind-hearted and loving brother of mine. You are so divine. Send my deepest love and remembrance to dearest sister Mary Parry.

*

Poona 28 March 1969

Dear brother Fred,

Beloved Baba dropped his physical body to live forever and ever in our Baba hearts. Hold fast to Him my Beloved Father and Mother, Compassionate One, Avatar Meher Baba.

Thanks for sending me your loving gift of five pounds. I shall always cherish your love and kindness. Are you going to come to Poona for Darshan - let me know if so, I'll be too glad to meet you again?

With much love and remembrance in the Infinite.

Your loving brother,

Jal

***

Dr. W. Donkin

Donkin first met Baba in 1933 at the home of Kitty Davy, having come to know of Him through Will Backett. On completion of his medical training, he went to serve Baba in 1939 'in whatever manner Baba chose'. He barely left India thereafter, and died just six months after Baba Himself, some said of a broken heart.

Following is a letter to Will Backett transcribed by Fred into a notebook. It was sent when Dr. Donkin was serving in the Indian Medical Service during WWII, and hence frequently away from Baba. It reads as an intimate 'Baba family catch up' letter and Will shared 'India news' with Fred. As this specific period of his life is not referenced in *Donkin's Diaries* or *Slave of Love*,[*7] and includes Mast stories, I record it in its entirety as the content makes interesting reading.

Letter from Capt. William Donkin, I.M.S, 14 October 1944

I don't see much of Baba these days except whenever I can get leave every few months, and I was in Dehra Dun for three weeks in August, seeing Baba every day and hope to see him again at the end of this month.

In spite of all hints to the contrary, he still does a lot of mast work, and those whom he can take with him to where he is staying, he does, doing the usual bathing, feeding and so on. You will of course remember Mohammed, the mast who was in Cannes. About a year ago, he said he wanted to leave Baba, and so went to Bombay, where he was looked after by Ali, the hero of *Sobs and Throbs.*[*8] The latter is now a materially inclined fellow in a restaurant business. Lately, Mohammed, after spending some months at Ratnagiri on the West Coast, (his old home) decided to come back to Baba, and now he is with Him at Lonavla.

Actually, the real cream of the masts was an old Chatti Baba of whom I think I sent you a photo some while ago. You may have met Eruch Jessawala. He does a good deal of mast work with Baba, and the following tale of his is interesting. You know that when Baba works with the masts, He shuts himself in a room with them and allows no one else in. Just before Baba left Bangalore in April 1940, He tried to get Chatti Baba to sit with Him for half an hour in His hut in the *Links* compound. Chatti Baba refused repeatedly, being rather childish, liking to keep himself to himself.

Eventually on the very eve of Baba going away with us all, Chatti Baba, of himself, came to Baba's hut, and said he would sit with Baba. They were alone in the hut for about an hour, and at the end of it Chatti Baba rattled on the door to be let out and Eruch, who was on guard outside, went to unlock the door. Eruch, being a fattish and phlegmatic sort of chap, not expecting anything or being sensitive or anything, says that as Chatti Baba came out, he felt a powerful and painful electric shock, which upset him for a moment. Baba of course always says that these masts help him in His work, so doubtless the sparks fly a bit when they get together, and Chatti Baba was said to be a sixth plane mast, a pir[*9] in fact.

While I was at Dehra Dun, Baba sent me to see all the places at Hardwar and Rishikesh, including the bungalow where they had all been. You would have loved these famous Hindu Pilgrim centres, at Rishikesh, where the Ganges comes sweeping out of the Himalayas, a grey rushing turbulent river, with cool water from the glaciers in the Himalayas with Kardan Bandrinath 100 miles away. The hills on each side rise 6-7,000 feet, covered with trees up to the summits.

Hardwar, (God's door), 15 miles below Rishikesh, is a great place in the traditional Hindu style, with bathing ghats, temples, etc, a very colourful and fascinating place. Baba was in a very good mood while I was in Dehra Dun, plenty of jokes and talks about his school days, with funny incidents. He is really very active these days, and of course keeps on rushing off on mast tours all over India. On these tours there are often a lot of funny incidents, Gustadji usually goes too, and what with Gustadji's finger language and Baba's nods, they usually cause some inquisitiveness on the trains. At one station someone insisted that Baba had come there to find a brother he had lost. In spite of denials, the man insisted that this was so - he said he could read faces and knew it to be true. After about half an hour, about 40 people collected around Baba and party on the platform, every newcomer being told this false tale, so people giving great sympathy to Baba at the loss of His brother.

Another time in a train, Baba was told that He ought to go and take Darshan of a famous Saint at Ahmednagar called Meher Baba! Another time Baba insisted on bargaining over some oranges on a station stall where there was a picture of Himself. The man held Him in great esteem but did not recognise Him in the flesh when He came to bargain over oranges at the station stall with him!

Aga Baidul, whom you all remember, is the chief mast finder at present, as Kaka is mostly with his sister in Bombay. As for Meherabad, the track which goes up the Hill from the railway, has now got young trees on either side, which in 30 years' time will be very pleasant indeed. Down the Hill is much the same as before, very pleasant these months, (I saw it last in August), with the crops growing up.

The Dhuni, or sacred fire, is still lit monthly, as when started last December, by Baba's orders. It is lit just at the side of that wooden Hut by the roadside, in which Baba wrote His books, years ago. In those days, there was a special fire there, constantly burning. The neem tree by the Hut, has been struck by lightning, but is still living well. The garden up the hill is very good now, with plenty of flowers and trees growing well.

Another time in a train, Baba was told that He ought to go and take Darshan of a famous saint at Ahmednagar called Meher Baba! Another time Baba insisted on bargaining over some oranges on a station stall where was a picture of Himself. The man held Him in great esteem, but did not recognise Him in the flesh when He came to bargain over oranges at the station stall with him.

Aga Baidul, whom you all remember, is the chief mast finder at present, as Kaka is mostly with his sister in Bombay.

As for the Meherabad, the track which goes up the hill from the railway, has now got young trees on either side which in thirty years time will be very pleasant indeed. Down the hill is much the same as before — very pleasant, these months, (I saw it last in August) with the crops growing up.

The monthly "Dhuni" or sacred fire is still lit monthly, as when started last December, by Baba's orders. It is lit just at the side of that wooden hut by the roadside, in which Baba wrote His books years ago. In those days, there was a special fire there, constantly burning... The "Neem" tree by the hut, has been struck by lightning, but is still living well. The garden up the hill is very good now, with plenty of flowers and trees growing well.

Nasik, which I saw last in August too on my way back from Dehra Dun, is in good form — the Meher Retreat is rather vacant with Rustam gone, and only the old lady in the main bungalow. Occasionally people use those rooms, but they are getting out of repair. The garden on the other hand has got very good in the last two years. Ramju and Dr Ghani, whom I saw are in good form. Ramju's son is to marry Ghani's daughter soon. Padri is now in Deolali, near Nasik, doing some motor business on Baba's orders. He wants to go back to Meherabad.

Sample page of Dr Donkin's letter.

Nasik, which I saw last on August 2 on my way back from Dehra Dun is in good form, the Meher Retreat is rather vacant with Rustom gone and only the old lady in the main bungalow. Occasionally people use those rooms, but they are getting out of repair. The garden on the other hand has got very good in the last two years. Ramjoo and Dr Ghani, whom I saw are in good form. Ramjoo's son is to marry Ghani's daughter soon. Padri is now in Deolali, near Nasik, doing some motor business on Baba's orders. He wants to go back to Meherabad. I am still in Bangalore, but now Adi and Ghani have gone from here, so I miss their company. The Byramangala Centre is still as it was, but the Big Lake behind, which is being made by the construction of a huge dam, is filling up with water, and the place will be very beautiful later on with this lake there. I go out there about once a month, just to see all is OK. A Mohammedan caretaker is looking after it. I have now risen to the dignity of Captain in the I.M.S, but always itch for the time when I can join Baba again, as soon as the war is over.

Well a Very Merry Xmas and New Year to you both and the 'old stagers', and here's to Baba's Day when peace and genuine friendship and understanding are paramount again in a new, and as we feel, a better world.

Yours ever, Donkin

This concludes a sample of Fred's extensive correspondence over the decades of his life with Baba, but it is not comprehensive. To the casual observer, Fred's ascetic life may have appeared 'stripped to the bone', but what is reflected through these letters alone is a life rich and diverse in intimate contacts with Baba's family and close ones.

***

Shireen Bonner:

Shireen Bonner, the daughter of Adi and Franey Irani, who now resides in New Mexico, has kindly shared her memories of Fred from her childhood living in London, when her father worked with Fred.

I don't know for certain, but assume that my parents met Fred through Delia, Will and Mary Backett, *et al.* I also assume that my father at least had met him in India, but am not sure. My parents moved to England in 1956. Fred and my father struck up a friendship with a shared interest in antiques. My dad ran an antiques shop in Hammersmith (I think) and I believe that Fred was either in partnership, or helped or advised him. Not at all sure of details.

In any case, Fred was the main person amongst a few others who encouraged my father to go into the antiques business, which he continued for the rest of his life. Fred was a real fixture in our lives - we saw him all the time. He came to the Baba meetings. I'm fairly certain and would often visit us; and at one point, he lived in our garden shed! It then seemed that Fred and our family might have lost touch - did he move away from London? Towards the end of his life, when he was living in a small bedsit - perhaps some sort of assisted living - my mum, who was endlessly kind, would regularly take meals and food to him and would visit him until the very end.

I wish that I could tell you more. I do know that my dad was very fond of Fred. Personally, whenever I watch the film *Three Incredible Weeks* with the men filing past in front of Baba, and Fred kneels in front of Him, I'm always moved.

Appendix 2 - English Arti and Creative Writing

Fred liked poetry, and sometimes copied lines of Kabir or Hafiz. He also penned his own, found scattered randomly through his notes. The couplets that have appeared as Chapter headings were extracted from an extended piece of Fred's poetry. For brevity I include a few of his poems - an ardent student could refer to Friends of MBA, UK to read them all.

Fred also loved singing and playing the piano, favouring old hymns. He learnt the national anthems of many countries during the war years. Later he wrote an English Arti at Baba's request, and sometimes encouraged visiting Baba lovers to sing it with him, accompanied by Lol Benbow on guitar.[*1] Lol remembers it thus:

Fred had chosen an English hymn tune which was new to me, and we agreed how the words would fit to the melody with only one adjustment to the text. No other changes allowed. He had composed this Arti at Baba's request via Olive Pitt who had 'inner conversations' with Baba over many years. The Arti is based on Hafiz's *[poetic style]* from an old book Fred had. He was old when I met him and his voice was very wavery – one time he was singing something to me and I couldn't tell which note he was going for, the higher or the lower. We giggled.

Though sung infrequently at Baba's Samadhi, the Arti was 'resurrected' by Keith Ashton and Phil Simpson[*2] at the memorial for Lol Benbow in November 2022, sung to a familiar hymn tune. I hope someone makes a recording while it remains in their memory since no recording exists.

English Arti

Oh Meher, this pledge I owe to You.
My life - no longer can I renew,
At long last you have come to redeem
This life I owe, I give and yield to You.

Heaven's favour made me ask my way to Thee.
Eternal guidance led me Your face to see,
Yet passing by You paid no heed to me
Though my heart opens to a Guest like Thee.

Oh Meher, Grace can blend this heart of mine
So, make it pure by Thy Love Divine,
I stand suppliant at Thy door,
And crave to beg for more and more.

Deep down within I'll be worthy of Your trust,
Otherwise, mindful I am but dust.
That each day, in all I think or do or say,
Shall give repose at the end of day.

O Meher, accept this song of praise
Since when my life renews its gaze,
The arrow of Your Love strikes my heart again,
Each day Your praise I study to proclaim.

The theme of life's solace is Your dear Name.
The moments fly but I repeat the same,
If I'm united with Meher in my heart
No matter if we are placed far apart.

The hold of Your Daaman I'll ne'er consent to part,[*3]
With many tears You've been purchased by this heart,
So, love Baba, no living thing distress,
This is the way to God and happiness.

May the Object of my heart unfold my life,
My soul and spirits joy behold!
For young and old, as far as climes extend,
Must in some urgency require a friend.

O Glorious Saviour of Ancient Might
Bear me on to realms of endless Light,
When the last veil of night is drawn
My soul arises at the glorious dawn.

Surely Meher Baba is worthy of All Praise
Lord of Creation, The Ancient of Days,
His seven-coloured banner high above unfurls,
In fullness and Glory, He sways the three worlds.

***

Love

Love is motiveless but motivates all.
The life of the spirit moves to the 'Call'.
Love is like the sun shining on leaf and flower,
Motiveless, the gentle breeze gives movement to
the quivering leaf –

And movement to the swaying flower.
Love gives birth to life renewed,
And motivates man to selfless deeds –

In tender care to the heart that bleeds.

All is Love and Love is All –
Is all that motive needs.
The real death is self - forgotten.
Love is life and is in dying.
Love does not test, but 'Is' the test
that bends the strong –
and gives strength to the weak.

Love moves all things into motion –
Inspiring man for purest devotion – and
The life of the spirit is in loving deeds,
In selfless service for another's needs.
While mighty ambition grinds to test
The sinews and minds of the struggling rest

Where there is no love, no worth is gain,
Such motives drive but do not sustain.[*4]

***

Untitled

Greatness comes not from service or from skill,
But from the mandates of the Eternal Will.
In memory of the Beloved's face, our solitude we
prize,
That Love has freed us from the world and snapped
all other ties.

What matter though in travel's path the thorn of
trouble grows -
Since from this thorn I gather, every moment,
pleasure's rose.
Oh! I recall the time when near Thy dwelling was
my stay.
Now I would my eyes were brightened by the dust of
Thy doorway!
Ask me not what woes of love, what pangs have
been my lot,
All the griefs that parting brings I've tasted – ask me
not!
Oh! nightingale that with the rose dost sit,
They state is blissful, therefore value it.
Behold this wondrous flower, which has blossomed
here for me –
Its colour cannot be imagined, nor its fragrance
hidden be.
Reproaches shall not drive me from His door.
Since I inhaled Thy fragrance on the morning gales,
News from my loved one – happy news – inhales.
Here branches of sweet shrubs this fragrance gave,
And here tall trees, their graceful foliage wave.
The hyacinth, the cypress foot attends,
The violet before the lily bends.[*5]

***

Feed My Lambs –

Found in Fred's 'late life' notes, his thoughts on Baba's injunction to him to 'Feed My Lambs'.

<u>Feed My Lambs.</u>

The greater the number of aspirants gathered in a group, the less it would seem becomes the intimacy by which the aspirant or seeker is enabled to unburden his or heart. It follows more so when formalities arise and take precedence. ·····

The masterpiece, 'God Speaks' is a volume Baba insisted all should read, even though it might not be readily understood. However after careful perusal the contents gradually become mentally constructive as sentences correlate to each other and blend for the aspirant's understanding. Even if not understood the volume 'God Speaks' forms a base for the understanding of the Discourses etc,. 'God Speaks', is the only book which outlines in constructive detail the creation and the spiritual forces which sustain and maintain it at every level. Its inherent spiritual potency is yet to enlighten and vitalize sleeping Humanity, appeasing and answering man's intellectual capacity to absorb and so brings to bear on his spiritual destiny.

In this life time we have come into incarnation with a heavy burden of credit and debit of factors, and although mercifully they do not have to be accounted for, if however the mind and heart are put to balance, the heart is left with a heavy deficit.

Baba has come to our rescue to help restore the lost balance between heart and mind, in respect of which, Baba meetings play an important role. Baba has come to sow the seed of Love in the heart of man. It is God's gift to mankind and as Baba lovers, we are entrusted to help through His Grace to live and share in the God-given task in winning our fellow-human beings over to the Love of God.

Towards this end the intellect must be weighed in the scales of service and gradually coaxed into sub-mission if the heart is to come into play, and benefit all the seekers, ~~and~~ aspirants, and new-comers present at a Baba meeting.

The intellect as a servant gradually becomes purified in the the life of the spirit. In this role it becomes subservient to the heart and a leverage in all discussions. The heart has become stifled and our intellect is ever ready to assert itself and offer some sort of answer to our own or another's problem, though it may not be the right answer. The ingredients which go to the make-up of the mind, do not easily respond to our spiritual aspirations, having in mind that the ingredients of the intellect comprises a combination of experience, reading, logic and dogma. Through those factors we have maintained a strong-hold on Ignorance.

Nonetheless the intellect does lend itself to convey for one's enjoyment a glorious sunset or the beauties of nature, and as a means for discrimination it plays a major role in the art of living. In the realm of creativity, the intellect helps man to survey and explore such possibilities as the theme of creation. By this is not meant the 'exploring of planetary space'.

But the unredeemed loneliness of the heart cannot find a remedy in aesthetic or ethical values for its fulfillment. It requires humility to allow the heart to express itself through the over-powering mind.

But divine Love transforms and sets at nought our ignorance as light steals across and darkness ceases to be.

contin:

"Divine Love is matchless in Majesty. It has no parallel in power, and there is no darkness it cannot dispel."

(discourses - Meher Baba.

And so the intellect, so apt to calculate egotiscally must align itself to other resources re-discovered when the devotee takes a stand towards spiritual service if the heart is to be allowed expression. The intellectual faculty has a simile, such as in the purpose which serves as the framework of a crown, which upholds in its setting, the facetted and priceless jewels which shine in lustre and send out rays beyond their setting.

Christ instructed His Apostles, and an injunction He commanded was that they were to "Feed My Lambs". The same divine mystical expression was sent to two of Baba's early disciples in England. "Feed My Lambs"! By that is to be understood that Baba would have His children given spiritual sustenance - 'Panis Angelica' - Bread of Heaven'!

He gives each one a tiny measure of Himself, redeeming the heart and mind and the quest gains momentum within each soul. When such experience becomes one's own it is priceless and beyond questioning. It is contagious, neither can it be measured in potency and increases when shared with others! It is eternal. It follows then that a meeting held in Baba's name can serve as a channel where each one attending should feel renewed in heart and mind - a content of spirituality, joy or peace of mind, uplifted and equipped for some sort of aspiration to fertilize his or her daily round of common tasks. It is great and ennobling, when a Baba lover so charged by Baba's grace goes into the world sharing

among his fellow-human beings the 'treasure' which
Baba brings. Every day becomes new, and what an
adventure!
I was present in India when Baba said:
  'What is a meeting? Baba replied: 'When
  two meet.'
At another time He said': 'The best meeting place is
under a tree.'

P.S. Baba often chose an open space, sometimes under a
  tree. Baba sat by a tree on a mound when He gave
  a sermon. Jesus gave a sermon on a mount.
  In England, John Wesley and other evangelists used
  open spaces. The Apostles likewise.

The King's Fortress - a play by Fred

Fred's play was kindly drawn to my attention by Scott
Makeig who directed a production of it for Baba's Birthday in
Berkeley, California in 1972. For this production, Scott set to
music lyrics Fred had written for a song and a children's
chorus. Writing about the play in a letter dated 21st January of
that year, Fred had said:

> This play is written in a dramatic idiom, a
> harmony of emotion Baba liked, but then Beloved
> liked the songs of the age. The songwriters had
> beautiful words to express, in the rhythm of the age,
> the best that came to mankind - often prior to the

Coming of the Incarnation, at His birth, youth, and onwards. We enter a new age of idiom, sound, harmony, and rhythm, so the new must come gradually through Baba lovers whether dancing, poetry, or music. Baba liked the rhythm of the dancing at Myrtle Beach, (Margaret Craske's ballet dancers), but that was of the bygone or passing classical age.

Baba lovers must express their love to Beloved through loving inspiration, which is spontaneous, and not calculated thinking, simply just childlike grace. Some lovers can spontaneously sing and play instruments. It cannot come by coercion. Baba said to me, jot down thoughts during the night-time. It is growth. 'The New Testament', which has not yet come to the fore, is available. 'The New Testament' includes all, everything you young Baba lovers need, wherever you are. In it, the mystical of Beloved's teaching make glad the heart and mind of the lover. Beloved Master helps us to express our love in the way He chooses for each one. The play is in the shadow light and glorious future portent. Beloved is awakening lovers to express their love for Him. Be happy in Baba - in His keeping.

The following script includes the stage directions that Fred thought appropriate to each scene, and to set the mood of the performance.

The King's Fortress.

Before rehearsing this play, participants, should repeat Baba's name either audibly or silently for 5 minutes.

Scene 1

Curtain rises. The door of a house with nameplate *Sleepy Valley*. Also, a garden or 'wayside seat' facing audience, right hand side of stage. Church bells chime 3:00 in the morning. Stage in semi-darkness. Light focussed on nameplate of door. Young man sits doubled or crouched with head in hands, bound loosely from head to foot in cellulose strips and coloured ribbons of paper (sanskaras). After six minutes the curtain falls.

Scene 2

Same as above but young man has withdrawn inside. Time 6:00 in the morning, break of dawn (light effects). Birds begin to sing, clock chimes 6 hours. Milk delivery boy arrives whistling tune, leaves milk bottle foot of door, first knocking twice on door, no reply. He then chalks on side of door: 'Fellow traveller, do not weep, they are not dead but fast asleep.'

Milk boy quickly departs, and whistles tunes to the above lines. From backstage a female singer repeats tune, and refrain is taken up in variations by chorus of girl singers repeating several times.

Interval of two to three minutes.

Postman arrives, knocks three loud knocks, places letter through letterbox, reads the chalk notice and smiles. Postman turns away. Softly the refrain is repeated backstage. He pauses, listens, then quickly departs.

Interval of two minutes.

Door opens from within sufficiently for hand to appear and lift the bottle of milk. The door closes quietly. The curtain falls.

Interval during which *Plaisir d'Amour* is played, sung by Paul Robeson – Beloved Baba had this record played to Him in India, September, 1954.

Scene 3

Same set as before. Time is 3:00 early morning. Stage in semi-darkness. The young man appears wearing black cloth with coloured ribbons winding around him, and moves on steadily towards door, tries key in door, finds it barred, then knocks, and finally tries the doorknob. He appears desperate, shrugs his shoulders, buries his head in the palm of his hands and assumes the previous position at the doorstep where he falls asleep.

(The effect of dawn is given by lighting in gradual stages). People go hurriedly to work passing to and fro in front of the house. First a police officer who pauses and takes a glance towards the doubled-up figure, then proceeds across stage, then quickly follow office workers. A little girl going to school carrying a school satchel swings along quickly, notices the figure and pauses, then runs away off stage.

Curtain closes.

Scene 4

The figure of the young man is not present. Birds are singing. Same setting, very sunny day. Light focused upon woman sitting on bench. As the curtain rises, she appears perfectly still, absorbed in reading a book. She has pleasant appearance. After three-minute silence the young man appears, tries to enter through the door but finds it locked. He lowers his head, and with emotion says, "Oh God".

The woman does not appear to notice the figure, closes the book, and rising from the bench commences to leave. Refrain from backstage in sweet-sounding voice sings song: "Spare a moment," etc.

The chorus joins in with the singer. The woman pauses and turns facing the audience. From the other side of the stage a male voice in deep and clear tones is heard reciting: "The speech of one heart-troubled is hard, (pauses, continues softly), the rapture, water, cloud-like sorrow comes to his eyes."

The young man faces the audience and utters to himself: "This pleasure of wine lasts but for five days!"

The woman slowly turns her head and takes one step towards him and is on the point of speaking with a kind gesture. The young man, sensitive to the gesture, reacts quickly and says loudly: "What need to me of anyone's advice, (continues with dramatic emotion) this very need is sufficient to me!"

He clenches his fist with his right hand and strikes his left breast in anguish and says to himself more subdued – "The sound of the harp becomes weak through the drum!"

For effect the audience hear a faint sound of a harp and drum. He now turns towards the woman, asks her pardon, notices the book she holds and quietly says, "Lady, may I ask what the book is you are holding?"

The woman smiles but hesitates to reply. Then the refrain is sung and heard from the singers at the back of the stage. "Spare a moment, pause awhile...." etc.

She now opens the book at the title page and photograph of Meher Baba. The young man's face lights up as he reads aloud.

"Avatar Meher Baba - I have come not to teach but to awaken".

He pauses and raises his head, again pauses, and steps forward towards the audience. Backstage is heard the recording of '*Ah sweet mystery of life, at last I've found Thee*' (Cole Porter[**]). The first verse gradually fades away. The young man takes another step forward, and in a clear soft voice begins to recite the following verses. Gradually stage lights focus on him, and the woman disappears off stage.

> "I seem to hear strange music like none I've heard before
>
> Comes floating softly earthwards through heavens open door.
>
> Now soft and low and restful, it floods my soul with peace,
>
> As if God's benediction bade all earth's troubles cease."[*6] (pause)

At the end of the last line the singers, male and female, and musicians blend in the music of the song Baba had played to him in India, September 18th, 1954, as follows:

[At this point Fred, misremembering possibly, inserts a close approximation of the lyrics of a song from an Edwardian musical. The song, *Ah, Sweet Mystery of Life*, was not written by Cole Porter, but by Rida Johnson Young (lyrics) and Victor Herbert (music)[**]. Fred has it beginning thus:

> "Ah sweet mystery of life, at last I found thee,
> Now at last I know the secret of it all."]

Finale: The Children's Chorus accompanied by tubular bells –

"Joy bells ringing, birds are singing, fill the air with music sweet,

Joyful measure of love's treasure makes the chain of song complete.

Earth seems brighter, hearts grow lighter, charming sadness into gladness.

Skies are clearing, and we're hearing Joy bells ringing everywhere."[*7]

***

Appendix 3 - Obituary

This heart is for loving and for Baba to illume,
every other thing I strive to consume.
To this end my life I'll expend,
and when called to depart,
I'll give and yield with mind and heart.

Fred passed on 2ⁿᵈ March 1985. On hearing the news, a telegram was sent from Meherazad on Wednesday 6ᵗʰ March:

> Dear Fred has gone home to his precious Lord Avatar Meher Baba, after life lived totally in Beloved Baba's service. We know that all hearts he had lighted with Meher Baba's Love will miss this 'Grand Old Man' of England but will rejoice in his well-earned joy and bliss of reunion with the Lord.
>
> Avatar Meher Baba. Ki Jai.
>
> from Mehera, Mani, all Mandali

In a memorial Newsletter circulated by Meher Baba Association after Fred's passing, Lol Benbow wrote as follows:

> Fred Marks - 6th January 1900 - 2nd March 1985
>
> On March 2nd in early morning, our dear Fred Marks passed away at the Royal London Homeopathic

Hospital, Great Ormond Street, London. Fred had not kept well since he gave that wonderful Baba-filled talk to us at Hammersmith Grove, on November 10th, 1984, demonstrating his love and attunement to his Beloved Baba. The last few months he had been looked after devotedly by his close group.

To many, a sweet old gentleman, to some an inspiring example, and a truly gentle man. To those who knew him well, a selfless servant of his Beloved, and Baba's "very good boy". Fred was a true mystic. His perspective on life reflected this and he was not always understood as a result.

Outwardly, his life was 'filled with people', his roles varying from service in the Guards (from which he bought himself out), to art dealer, gardener at a remand home, and school master at a large public school. He became sick of his worldly life and gave away his wealth realizing his true spiritual longings on seeing Lord Jesus during the Second World War. When he met Meher Baba, The Master told him, "You know who I am."

But inwardly, Fred was a very private person, with fiercely held views and very independent. He once told me that simple thoughts were the most powerful, and judging by his example, pertinent and easily grasped comments revealed his penetratingly beautiful perceptions of the underlying truth to be found everywhere. He was a simple man, delighting in nature and tranquillity, a beacon of peace and surrender to the Will of his Beloved. Believing that it is one of the hardest things to help another, he advocated a kind word, a smile and silence as a comfort to those in distress. So very many knew him as a comforter, and as a true lover of Meher Baba with the common touch, his pure wish was to whisper for only Baba to hear, "Darling, I love you!" He is now safely in His arms forever

***

Anne Collette, a long time French Baba lover living in London said of Fred:

I only remember and cherish the feeling of Meher Baba's Presence through Fred, profound love and devotion bringing Baba so close and so vividly present, like a soft light emanating from him.

Appendix 4 – Epilogue

You the reader may have reached the end of this book still wondering who Fred really was. The sheer absence of personal detail, considering how many encountered him, all with exclusively positive recollections, is something of an enigma. Few recall Fred sharing anecdotes about himself. Most remark on his humility, a quality so exceptionally rare in the Western world where so many seek the spotlight.

Was Fred quietly modelling self-effacement; was he consciously erasing all sense of himself; had whatever ego he once had all but disappeared by the time our memory-bearers met him? Can we rightly describe him as a Christian Mystic? What is remarkable about his seemingly unremarkable life is that it was supremely rare. Fred was chosen in his time from the 50 million souls incarnate in the UK, and from billions of souls in the universe, to serve the Lord of the Universe and Avatar of the Age while He was present on earth. This alone is surely worthy of contemplation.

Fred survived two World Wars, having declared to someone privately that Baba had saved his life on three occasions. That he only hints at those experiences may speak volumes. He knew poverty and solitude for most of his life, but did not appear to experience theses as defining attributes.

He believed he had acquired the Treasure beyond all treasures, and enjoyed the company of the court of the King.

Where does he fit in the 'canon of souls' who have surrendered their lives to Beloved Baba? Is there significance in his life lived without apparent hurt or harm to others, where no discernible footprints remain, barely a trace of presence, and yet ripples that still flow gently and quietly on, as when a breeze stirs the surface of a lake?

I had no personal attachment to Fred or reason to write his biography, I simply felt impelled, and others were enthusiastic and encouraging. It seems Baba wanted, indeed wants, Fred's life witnessed, and in that shared witnessing perhaps He is offering us the challenge to know and experience Him as Fred did - quietly, inwardly and wholeheartedly without any fuss or outward show, yet with complete conviction. A simple man living a simple life, unhesitatingly approaching his Beloved to fulfil his ultimate wish to whisper in His ear, Darling, I love You!

***

Endnotes

Introduction

1. Friends of Meher Baba, UK, often referred to as MBA, (the Meher Baba Association, UK) is based at Flats 1&2, 228 Hammersmith Grove, London, W6 7HG.

(email: *mbaboard@yahoo.com - www.meherbaba.co.uk*)

Part One

Chapter One – Early Years

1. "The term 'Providence' is an expression commonly used to explain some singular instance, timely care or provision, or control of God over His creatures. Such incidents happening in the life of a person are commonly referred to as 'luck', 'providential' or 'fortunate'. Because the ego stands in the way, such an incident may be ignored. On the other hand, it may be looked upon as auspicious." - Fred's subtext clarification.

2. 91st Psalm of David, *King James Bible*

3. A Moveable Feast, Ernest Hemingway, pub. Scribner's (USA), Jonathon Cape (UK), 1964

4. A loose translation of the Pavamana Mantra or ancient prayer introduced in the Brihad-Aranyaka Upanishad. Fred's source is not known. Reference used: *The Upanishads,* translated by Juan Mascaro, Penguin Classics, 1965. pp 127

5. This text is known as *The Sarum Primer*, one of the earliest recorded Christian prayers, believed to have been developed in Salisbury in the 13th Century, but first published in 1558.

6. Christian Hymn authored by Edwin Hatch 1835-1889, published posthumously in *Towards Fields of Light*, London, 1890.

7. Fred does not clarify how Madame Polli recognised Baba, but maybe, like himself, it was from newspapers, or maybe through her contact with Will and Mary Backett. When this incident was mentioned to Adi Sheriar Jnr., Baba's youngest brother, almost nineteen years later, he told Fred that he was accompanying the Master with another member of the Mandali, Adi K Irani, at the time. Madame Polli apparently had a similar resemblance to his mother Shireenmai.

8. Meher Baba directed that in the future a Memorial Tower should be built at Meherabad incorporating names of those who have 'served My cause with unimpeachable integrity of character' and in the future... 'who set aside thoughts of self and make their life an offering to the divine and imperative cause of the Master.' Baba laid the foundation Himself on 23rd December 1944, and the Tower was inaugurated 23rd December 2019.

9. Lord Meher, Bhau Kalchuri, *pp.3125*

Chapter Two – Will and Mary Backett

1. This was a much more profane song which originated around the late 18th early 19th century as a marching song, about the abolitionist John Brown, and was popular during the American Civil War.

2. Babajan, who was one of the Five Perfect Masters, beckoned Baba one day in 1913 as He was passing. Thereafter He visited her regularly. In January 1914 she took Baba's face in her hands and, kissing His forehead, lifted a veil from His consciousness. From that moment He came to know his role as Avatar.

3. Meher Baba worked with many souls He contacted called, 'masts', who were souls intoxicated with their love for God.

Chapter Three – Meeting Meher Baba, 1952

1. I have tried without success to find the source of this quote in early Baba publications, as it resonates as if from Him. However, there is a publication, *God Calling* edited by A.J Russell, first published by Dodd, Mead & Co, 1945, now in its 25th edition. This publication is shrouded in mystery, having been compiled by two women who wished to remain anonymous. It has been read worldwide. Was one of them

Jean Adriel, or simply two agents of Baba? If any can enlighten me, please do.

2. *Ibid.*

3. *Meher Baba's Visits to England*, compiled by Margaret Hickman, published by Meher Baba Association, March 2001, pp 40

Chapter Four – Call to India, 1954

1. *The Awakener Magazine (Awakener),* Vol.2 No.4, Spring 1955 – Special Edition

2. Christian Hymn composed by Henry Twells, b.1823; composed in 1868.

3. *Fred Marks London 1971 – The Oral History Archive Project* – Irwin Luck Interview Series, YouTube (*www.youtube.com*)

4. *The God Man,* C.B.Purdom, Sheriar Press, 1964, pp252

5. *Meher Baba's Call,* edited by Chris Riger, 2011, narrated by Darwin Shaw, Sheriar Books. Darwin attended the '54 Darshan and was the author of *As Only God Can Love*, Sheriar Foundation, and the popular late-life collected writings *Effort and Grace, (www.Squarespace.com)*

6. *Three Incredible Weeks with Meher Baba*, edited by Robert Frederiks and narrated by Bill Le Page and Merwan Jessawala. Bill Le Page attended the '54 Darshan and lived at Meher Abode, Australia until his recent passing aged 98. Bill published many books on his Beloved Baba that can be sourced through *www.avatarsabode.com.au*

7. *Ibid.*

8. *www.ambppct* online library

9. *Three Incredible Weeks with Meher Baba*, Malcolm Schloss & Charles Purdom, Sheriar Books.

Chapter Five – Christian Mysticism

1. *King James Bible*, Matthew 9.29

2. *Ibid*, Matthew, 17.20

3. Sourced from Fred's Green Binder pp 1-2

4. Christian Hymn: *There is a Green Hill*, vs.4 by Cecil Frances Alexander (f), 1848

5. Sourced from Fred's Green Book with Red Binder pp 3-4

Chapter Six – Baba in London,1956

1. *Lord Meher* online, (*www.lordmeher.org*) pp.3975

2. *Ibid*, pp.3976

3. *Ibid*, pp.3982

4. *Meher Baba – Lord of Mercy,* pamphlet compiled by Fred Marks and loaned for the purposes of this book by Philip Creagar of Myrtle Beach.

5. *Much Silence,* Tom and Dorothy Hopkinson, Victor Gollancz, 1974, pp 113

6. Meher Baba quoted in *Meher Baba's Visits to England*, Margaret Hickman, Meher Baba Association, 2001

Chapter Seven – American Sahavas, July 1956 and May 1958

1. *The God Man,* C.B.Purdom, Sheriar Press, 1964, pp296

2. *Awakener, Special Sahavas Issue*, Vol 5, No.3, 1958 edited by Filis Frederik.

3. *Ibid*, Purdom, pp308

4. By the time this was written, Will would have been retired, and like Fred living on a modest income. The requested move from Kent to London would undoubtedly have resulted in a lowering of living standards, owing to differing property values and a higher cost of living in the capital.

5. Some have reported that Fred had previously been Saint Mark. Maybe Mary knew more than many, but this cannot be substantiated by the Editor.

6. Speaker's Corner is a location within Hyde Park, where traditionally anyone can freely take a stand and address whomsoever passes by, on any subject of their own choosing.

Chapter Eight – Filis Frederick

1. This, and all subsequent letters, now held in Fred's archive by Friends of Meher Baba, UK.

2. King James Bible, Psalm 136.1. This approximates to the oft-quoted Psalm. The exact notation is 'O give thanks unto the Lord; for he is good: for his mercy endureth forever.' Other editions, for example New American Standard Bible, include 'His loving kindness is everlasting'. We don't know which Bible Fred used, but it's likely to have been the King James Bible.

3. Life At Its Best, Meher Baba, Sufism Reoriented Inc., 1957

4. Meher Baba Lord of Mercy, compiled by Fred Marks (see Chapter Six)

5. See also *Glow*, Beloved Archives, Feb 1972 pp 29

Chapter Nine – Begin the Beguine

1. Begin the Beguine was composed by Cole Porter in 1935 while on the Cunard Ocean liner *Franconia*. It was introduced in October that year in the Broadway musical *Jubilee* at the Imperial Theatre in New York City.

2. This and subsequent correspondence shown was retrieved from a folder given by Marion Saunders to Keith Miles, two early UK Baba followers known personally to Fred.

3. Fred Marks at the London Baba Centre, 1984 - reproduced in *Awakener Magazine*, Vol 21 No.2, pp40

Chapter Ten – East West Gathering, 1962

1. Pandal – a large tented awning commonly used in India for large gatherings.

2. Awakener, Vol 9, Nos. 1 and 2

3. More Light, an Artist's Life with Meher Baba, Tom Riley, www.lifeofrileybooks.com, 2022.

Chapter Eleven – 'Pressing Forward'

1. Divya Vani Vol 1, No.2, August 1965. This was an Indian publication and Fred used to send articles to Adi Senior who then forwarded them to the editor for distribution.

2 & 3. Fred always avoided narrating his stories in the first person, never wanting to put himself in the spotlight.

4. In this context the meaning of 'regalia' means prerogatives, or special privileges of a sovereign, in this case Baba, the Sovereign of all.

Chapter Twelve – Fred's later life

1. This film can be viewed on *www.youtube.com* by searching Meher Baba - Fred Marks on Reincarnation.

Part Two – *Experiences*

1. Discourses, 7th Ed., pp373

2. By Meher Baba and described by Him as 'The Theme of Creation and Its Purpose'. Edited by Ivy O. Duce and Don E. Stevens, Sufism Reoriented, 1973

3. KJB, Matthew 25:40

4. Sanskaras – in Hindu philosophy, mental impressions or accumulated imprints of past experiences that determine one's present desires and actions.

5. Qutub-e-lrshid – Perfect Master

6. Listen Humanity, Meher Baba, narrated by Don Stevens, NY Harper and Row, 1971, pp187

7. Lord Meher online, pp 3301. Baba speaking in Dehra Dun, March 1953.

8. Discourses -7th Ed. pp 14

9. KJB, Galatians v1, 7-9

10. The Path of Love, Meher Baba, AMBPPCT, pp84-85

11. Meher Baba's Call, Discourse given out on 12th September, 1954

12. Sparks from Meher Baba, AMBPPCT, pp.21

13. This is one verse from a longer poem written by Alexander Pope, a neo-classicist, 1688-1744. It is commonly known as 'The Universal Prayer' written to ponder on the importance of empathy and showing mercy to others. It is likely that Fred knew this 'Universal Prayer' before he encountered Baba's Universal Prayer.

14. Lord Meher, Bhau Kalchuri, pp.5011

15. Christian hymn. Charles Wesley, 1747

16. KJB, 2 Corinthians, 12:9

17. I approached members of the Zoroastrian community to verify the accuracy of Fred's statement regarding the Prophet Daniel and the source of his quotes, but they could not be verified. I have chosen to include them as the content speaks to Fred's theme, and the two quotes have intrinsic beauty. I would welcome comment on their source from any reader.

18. Christian Hymn, 'The Day Thou Gavest Lord' by John Ellerton, 1870

19. Fred included a footnote in his journals referencing Matthew, Chapter 21, vs.42 – 'Jesus saith unto them, did ye never read in the scriptures, the stone the builders rejected, the same is become the head of the corner. This is the Lord's doing, and it is marvellous in our eyes'. The scripture Jesus was referring to is Isaiah 29:16 in the Old Testament. Further Fred relates 'our eyes' to 'the eyes Divine' referenced in Baba's Parvardigar Prayer given in September 1959.

20. Baba always referred to the five great Avataric religions: Hinduism, Zoroastrianism, Christianity, Islam and Buddhism. Some consider the domed roof of the Samadhi associates to the stupa of Buddhism, thus including the fifth faith path.

21. Bible, New Living Translation, Matthew 10:29-32

22. *Meher Baba Calling, No. 77*, Ed. Jamshed B.Mistry & J.Flagg Kris AMBPPCT, 1988

23. Baba's Universal Message, *The God Man,* C.B.Purdom, *pp.343-344*

Part Three - Appendices

Appendix 1 - Correspondence with Mandali and close disciples

(All correspondence held by Friends of Meher Baba Association, UK)

1. Meher Manzil was the London home of Baba's younger brother Adi and his wife Franey.

2. The spelling of Franey's name varied. In India Mani spelt it Franee, others Freni, but in later years, when Franey herself wrote from London, she signed her letters 'Franey'.

3. Sudam and Asha Wagh were Khorshed's caregivers who lived with her in the Trust compound.

4. Attributed to Allama Iqbal, (1887-1938) philosopher, politician and Urdu scholar.

5. Alan Cohen was one of three young American Baba followers, the others being Rick Chapman and Richard Dreyfus, whom Baba instructed to inform young people about the dangers of drugs and their use. They all gave countless public talks, sharing His messages after He dropped the body.

6. Watkins Books of London specialises in second-hand and antiquarian titles on mind, body and soul fields.

7. These are two wonderful biographies on the life of Dr. W. Donkin. *Donkin's Diaries* was compiled by Sarah McNeill, published by Sheriar Foundation, 2011. *Slave of Love* was compiled by Bob Mossman, Oceanic Publishing 2012

8. Sobs and Throbs, by Ramjoo Abdulla, AMB Phoenix Centre, 1964. This book describes Baba's work with boys in the Meher Ashram school.

9. In Islam, a saint or spiritual guide; in *God Speaks,* a soul on the 6th plane of consciousness.

Appendix 2 – English Arti and Creative Writing

1. Lol Benbow was a UK Baba follower and regular at Fred's meetings for many years.

2. Keith Ashton and Phil Simpson also had contact with Fred and were close friends of Lol's and helped to arrange his memorial service in 2022.

3. Daaman – the 'hem of a garment' of God.

4. Source – Green notebook, red binding.

5. Source – Loose leaf pages.

6. From *A Song of Heaven and Homeland*, a hymn by Eben Eugene M Rexford, USA, 1848-1916. Fred has combined couplets from separate verses to get his meaning across in the play.

7. From *Joy-Bells*, a hymn by Josephine Pollard, USA, 1834-1892.

*** *

Bibliography

Beams from Meher Baba, Ed. Ivy O. Duce, Sufism Reoriented, 4th Printing, 1996

Donkin's Diaries, Travels in India with Meher Baba, 1939-45, compiled and annotated by Sarah McNeill, Sheriar Foundation, 2011

Discourses, Meher Baba, Sheriar Press, Seventh Edition, 1987

Divya Vani, Ed. Swami Satya Prakash Udaseen, Avatar Meher Baba Mission, U.P. India

God Speaks: The Theme of Creation and Its Purpose, Meher Baba, Ed. Ivy O. Duce & Don E. Stevens. Second Edition, revised and enlarged, Dodd, Mead & Co., 1973

King James Bible, Authorised Version, Collins, 1956

Life at its Best, Meher Baba, Ed. Ivy O. Duce, Sufism Reoriented, 4th Printing, June 1974

Listen! The New Humanity, Don E. Stevens, Companion Books, 1985

Lord Meher: The Biography of Meher Baba, V.S.Kalchuri, North Myrtle Beach, South Carolina, Manifestation, 1986-2001. Online: *www.lordmeher.org/index.jsp.*

Love Alone Prevails, Kitty Davy, Sheriar Foundation, 2001

Meher Baba Calling, Eds. Jamshed B.Mistry & J. Flagg Kris, Meher Nazar Books, Ahmednagar, 5th edition, 1988

Meher Baba's Visits to England, compiled by Margaret Hickman, Sarsen Press, 2001

Much Silence, Meher Baba His life and work, Tom and Dorothy Hopkinson, London Victor Gollancz Ltd., 1974

Slave of Love, Bob Mossman, Oceanic Publishing, 2012

The Awakener Magazine, A Journal devoted to Meher Baba, Ed. Filis Frederick, 1953-1986 available online: *www.theawakenermagazine.org*

The God-Man, C. B. Purdom, Sheriar Press, 1971

The Path of Love, Meher Baba, Samuel Weiser, Inc, NY, 1976

The Silent Master Meher Baba, compiled by Irwin Luck, Meher Baba Archives Inc., 1987

The Silent Messenger, The Life and Work of Meher Baba, Tom and Dorothy Hopkinson, Mantra Books, 2019

The Upanishads, Trans. Juan Mascaro, Penguin Classics, 1965

Treasures from the Meher Baba Journals, Sheriar Press, 1980

Universal Dictionary, Collins, London and Glasgow, 1973

***

Baba answered Ned's question ' Is love beyond the form?'

Baba replied ' Infinite – infinite. At the same time Baba raised both His arms in gesture in emphasis.

Milton Keynes UK
Ingram Content Group UK Ltd.
UKHW041424201024
2278UKWH00015B/28